Fighting Through – From Dunkirk to Hamburg

Fighting Through – From Dunkirk to Hamburg

A Green Howard's Wartime Memoir

Paul Cheall: From the original story by Bill Cheall

This story is dedicated to the Green Howards

Pen & Sword
MILITARY

First published in Great Britain in 2011 by
Pen & Sword Military
An imprint of
Pen & Sword Books Ltd
47 Church Street
Barnsley
South Yorkshire
S70 2AS

ISBN 978 1 84884 474 2

A CIP catalogue record for this book is
available from the British Library

Typeset in 11pt Ehrhardt by Mac Style, Beverley, East Yorkshire
Printed and bound in the UK by the MPG Books Group

Pen & Sword Books Ltd incorporates the Imprints of
Pen & Sword Aviation, Pen & Sword Maritime, Pen & Sword Military,
Wharncliffe Local History, Pen & Sword Select, Pen & Sword Military Classics,
Leo Cooper, Remember When, Seaforth Publishing and Frontline Publishing

For a complete list of Pen & Sword titles please contact
PEN & SWORD BOOKS LIMITED
47 Church Street, Barnsley, South Yorkshire, S70 2AS, England
E-mail: enquiries@pen-and-sword.co.uk
Website: www.pen-and-sword.co.uk

Contents

Introduction

THIS IS a true story of an ordinary soldier in the Green Howards during the Second World War. The story includes, amongst others, my experiences at Dunkirk, D-Day, a voyage on the *Queen Mary* and being wounded in action.

Many of the events described in this book have been taken from notes written soon after those events took place. The remainder has been compiled from my memoirs which I set down more than forty years ago while they were still fresh in my mind and, more recently, I was given the inspiration to write everything down in book form so that other ex-servicemen may share some of the memories I have of that period in our lives.

Writing my memoirs gave me the opportunity to relive the years from 1939 to 1946. Looking back over the most traumatic and dare I say, exciting, time of my life causes me to delve very deeply into my thoughts and bring to the surface memories of things which happened so long ago that only a shadow remains; others have gone with the passage of time. However, some of the happenings are still so vivid in my mind that I can recall almost every detail.

What you are about to read is a true story of my service during the Second World War – nothing is invented or imagined. It is a story of events as I saw and experienced them and I will try, to the best of my ability, to describe vividly just how it was. At the beginning, little did I realize that my life would change forever as a result of my experience.

Come with me on a journey of reminiscence about: The 1939-45 Second World War.

Bill Cheall
4390717
May 1994

Postscript by the Editor

Dad's writing of this memoir was his way of telling his story to the family at a time when old soldiers generally didn't talk openly about their war exploits. I am so pleased that over twenty years after Dad first wrote his story, and eleven years after he died, others can now be entertained, enthralled and shocked by what Dad experienced, for without doubt the drama of this important historical script is remarkable.

Dad sincerely hoped our country would never again be as unready for war as we were in 1939 and if other people reading this book come to the same conclusion then his efforts will have been amply rewarded beyond that of having a family who are so very proud of him.

Paul Cheall

Note: A companion website exists for this book, with a wealth of background, links to various war graves, and the extending of individual people's stories when information becomes available. Even as I write, there have been some poignant discoveries which will be posted on the website. There are also many additional photographs of comrades and ephemera for which no space was available in the book. Go to www.fightingthrough.co.uk.

Prologue: Looking for Bray-Dunes

May 1940. Britain and her allies were at war with Germany. My B Company was part of the British Expeditionary Force in France. Germany had invaded the country and was now putting pressure on the Allied forces. We had orders to retreat to the coast to a place called Bray-Dunes, near Dunkirk, in order to evacuate back to England.

IT SEEMED to have taken a very long time but, after some hours and twelve miles, we saw a cluster of buildings in the distance and added a little more haste to our walking. We were surprised that our destination seemed no larger than a seaside village. Eventually, we came upon one main road through the centre of the village, rather shabby and uncared for, which was understandable. It looked just like Dodge City, but it was great to us. It was Bray-Dunes and we were very pleased to have sight of it but other troubles were very soon to descend upon us.

We walked down the sand-blown main street and at the end came to a small promenade overlooking the sea. Not a soul was in sight apart from our lads. We turned left and walked along this narrow promenade; it had a wooden rail along the seaward side, and there was a six-foot drop to the beach. We stood and looked at the sea which could mean our salvation – the other side of that water was England. Oh, that lovely sea, with England just on the other side – how simple!

We walked to the end of the promenade, about two hundred yards, which led on to deep soft sand, followed by huge, six-foot sandbanks. The sea was about two hundred yards away from the high water mark and both east and west the beach was very flat. The accompanying sight which greeted us will forever live in our memories. On the beach, running both ways, there were many tens of thousands of khaki-clad figures milling around for as far as we could see, but there was nowhere to go. And there were columns of soldiers, three-deep, going out to sea up to their shoulders trying to get onto the small boats to take them to England. It was 30 May.

I don't know how, but we made our way to the water's edge and looked out to sea across to the horizon and saw the ships going to Dunkirk, further along the coast. We then made our way back to the deep sand dunes in order to gain some protection from the bombing and strafing which was taking place. Many of the boys on the beach were in a sorry state; the Stukas had just been over.

One must remember that not all soldiers are hard-bitten individuals and some of the younger lads showed great emotion. I saw young soldiers just standing, crying their hearts out and others kneeling in the sand, praying. It is very easy to pass critical remarks about these lads, but we others knew the ordeal these weaker-willed boys were going through, and helped them as much as we could during their emotional and distressful ordeal as medical help was a very scarce thing on the beaches. So much had been bottled up inside these young soldiers that, at last, the bubble had burst and it was uncontrollable.

Dead soldiers and those badly wounded lay all over the place and many of the wounded would die. It was tragic to see life ebbing away from young, healthy lads and we could not do a thing about it – it was heartbreaking. What few stretcher-bearers there were always gave of their best – they were extraordinary. How does one quantify devotion to duty under the conditions which prevailed in those days? The folk at home could not possibly have any idea what their boys were going through.

There was no panic, just haste. We joined this mass of tired and hungry lads. Amidst all this tragedy, the Stukas would return, machine-gunning the full length of the thousands of men. They could not miss and a swathe of dead and wounded would be left behind; really it was awful, many of us fired our rifles at the planes, but they were useless. Nobody can imagine what it is like to be bombed by a German Stuka. They came out of the sky, screaming straight down, then dropped their bombs and pulled up into the sky again. I don't know why we ran – it was just instinct, I suppose.

Near the shoreline, one boy of about twenty not far from me had his stomach ripped open and he was fighting to live, asking for his mum and crying. A few of us went to him but he was too bad for us to help him; blood was everywhere. That poor boy soon died, out of pain, to join his mates. It is the most dreadful experience to see a comrade killed in such a way.

The near impossibility of getting back to England left many of us rather stunned, as it just did not look possible. Our lads, or what was left of our battalion, stuck together among the dunes to obtain some protection from the bombing and strafing. We had had nothing to eat except hard tack biscuits and bully beef – we hadn't had a hot meal for God knows how long and the lads who usually shaved looked really haggard.

None of us could see any sign of the 23rd Divisional assembly area and nobody seemed to know what to do for the best. Then the planes came over again, causing more deaths. Only twenty yards from me some lads had been hit by shrapnel and one of them was in a serious condition – the medics were there – but he would not live.

A sleepless night was ahead of us. There was no plan of action and even the officers seemed to be showing signs of tension. At about midnight we heard a plane coming, but it was not a bomber; it was dropping parachute flares and suddenly it was as light as day and eerie and fluorescent. Towards Dunkirk, there were dozens of fires caused by burning vehicles, and the flames from the burning oil storage tanks lit up the clouds. Very quickly, the Stukas came over doing their killing, flying the length of the beach, and we dug even deeper into the sand. Lads on the beach were running all over the place, but there was nowhere to go. I don't know why God was allowing this to happen, yet I saw so many boys praying to him, on their knees.

The morning eventually came and we were very cold, hungry and utterly miserable but there was no let up from our discomfort. I was beside Major Petch (I was his batman) and he said: 'Come along, Cheall, I want to see if I can find somebody in authority to give guidance to us.' From our elevated positions among the sand dunes we could see, more so, the thousands of soldiers on the beaches. Most of them, at this early hour, were lying around on the sand, certainly wondering what the day would bring; it would take a miracle for us all to be lifted off. I can't recall seeing any signs of despondency though; after all, we were soldiers, even if we were somewhat dishevelled and only showed natural tendencies to want to get out of the predicament we now found ourselves in. Oh, for a mess tin full of tea and, for most of the lads, a Woodbine!

Around 1100 hrs it looked as though officers on the beach were trying to organize the men. The Major and I went along the beach to try and find somebody with any news of what was happening about the evacuation. We had walked about one mile when we met our divisional commander, Major General Herbert. He was collecting a column of our 23rd Division in order to proceed to Dunkirk to try and get on a boat, since there was no chance of us being evacuated if we stayed where we were. He told Major Petch to collect his lads and join the column with utmost urgency. We hurried back to where our company was waiting to give them the news.

In the distance, we could see what must be Dunkirk. The five miles' walk there, tired as we were, seemed like fifty on the soft sand, which played havoc with tired legs. Ahead of us I could see the oil tanks with black smoke and flames pouring from them after they had been bombed. As we made our way along the beach, a fighter plane zoomed down to machine gun the men; many of us knelt down and fired with our rifles without any success.

We could see ships out at sea making their way from Dunkirk to England and could also see the dive-bombers after the ships. To our horror, many other ships had been sunk, their funnels and superstructures sticking out of the water – it was a ships' graveyard and it looked dreadful.

Eventually, our column reached the pier, or East Mole as it was called, and we waited in a long queue until it was possible for us to board a ship. Really, it is almost unbelievable, but even when we were attacked by planes we didn't move in case we lost our place in the column. The Mole was a wooden jetty only about five feet wide and one thousand four hundred yards long; it was never supposed to have large ships berth alongside.

Thousands of men had formed queues leading down to the sea and were in the water up to their shoulders, doing their utmost to get onto one of the small boats, which very often capsized. Beach masters had a very difficult task keeping some semblance of order, but by and large the lads just waited patiently for their turn to come until the planes came over. Those in the water just ignored the bombs – where could they run? And anyway, the sea absorbed a lot of the blast. There was always the hotheaded lad who thought he had more right to get away, but the officers only had to draw a revolver and they calmed down and accepted the inevitable. In the prevailing mood of many of the men it was common to see groups of soldiers kneeling down, being led by a Padre, in prayer.

There by the side of the jetty, a ship was waiting to be loaded with human cargo. We walked along the wooden pier and back came the planes – it seemed never-ending – trying to bomb our ship but without success. We walked along for about a half-mile to the ship we would be boarding. Miraculously, the Mole was still intact, but there was a six-foot gap in the planking where a bomb had gone through without exploding and loose planks had been put across. Some lads, in their desperate hurry, chose to jump the gap with their full kit on – luckily, none fell through into the water. Another thirty yards and we came to our ship. At the top end of a gangway stood an officer, counting soldiers as they went aboard.

The ship was a ferry ship called *The Lady of Mann* (how could I forget that name?). How lucky we considered ourselves to be; out of all those thousands of men, we were being given the opportunity to be evacuated. It was almost impossible for men of the same companies to stay together, but that was no consequence at a time like this.

The ferry was fast becoming packed with grateful lads. The Captain would know how many men the ship could carry, but God alone knows what would have happened had a bomb hit us! I was lucky enough to be on deck to see what was happening and it must have been very claustrophobic down below deck. I kept my eyes on the nearest Carley float in case the worst happened. The fact that we had managed to get on a boat was no guarantee that we would reach England because the Luftwaffe was doing its utmost to prevent us. As the ship was filling up, a Padre came and stood on a ladder, called for silence and prayed for our deliverance to England. At last, packed like sardines, the ship started to tremble and, so very slowly, we pulled away from the Mole – it was 1800 hrs, 31 May 1940.

Being a little taller than many of the lads enabled me to have a panoramic view of the whole length of the beach – how many of those boys would get back to England and how many would be killed or taken prisoner? The beach was as crowded as ever; then suddenly I saw a German fighter plane skimming above them, firing cannons – it reminded me of a row of dominoes being knocked down from one end.

The dense black smoke from the blazing oil storage tanks still reached far into the sky. There was another loaded ship about one mile ahead of us, and suddenly

I heard the Stukas returning, diving almost vertically. I saw the bombs leaving one of the planes and was certain our time had come, and that this was the end. My thoughts were mixed with prayer and despair as I prepared for what I thought was inevitable.

How the heck did it all come to this? As the bombs came tumbling out of the sky towards us, my life flashed before me and in an instant I relived every moment of my time since just before the start of the war, when life had seemed so good.

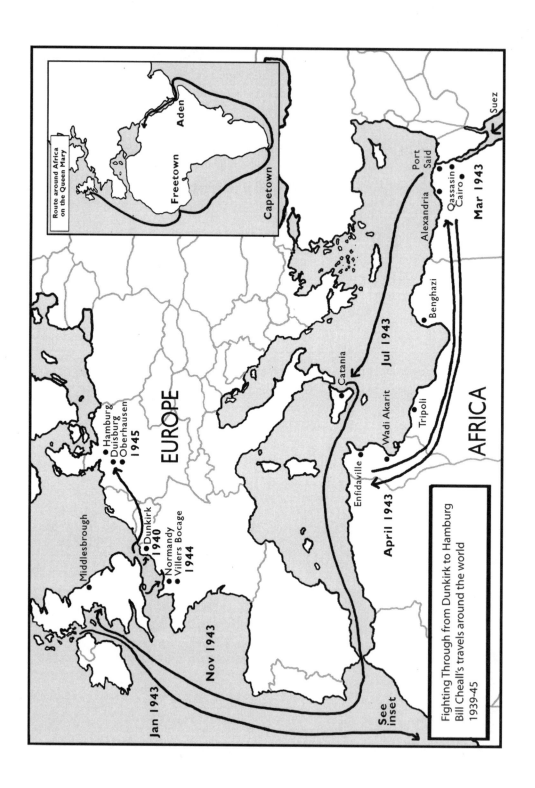

Route around Africa on the Queen Mary

Aden

Freetown

Capetown

Suez

Port Said

Alexandria

Qassasin
Cairo

Mar 1943

Benghazi

Catania

Wadi Akarit

Tripoli

Jul 1943

Enfidaville

April 1943

AFRICA

EUROPE

Hamburg
Duisburg
Oberhausen
1945

Middlesbrough

Dunkirk
1940

Normandy
Villers Bocage
1944

Nov 1943

Jan 1943

See
inset

Fighting Through from Dunkirk to Hamburg
Bill Cheall's travels around the world
1939-45

Chapter 1

The Beginning – The Territorial Army – 1939

IT WAS early April 1939, and a long cold winter lay behind us. It would soon be Easter, Spring was in the air and the notion, 'Put on your Easter bonnet, with all the frills upon it' helped to put everybody in a good mood, even though times were not too easy in 1939.

There was to be peace in our time, or so Neville Chamberlain, the Prime Minister, told us on his return from his meeting with Hitler. The good feeling at the start of spring belied the foreboding thoughts that were uppermost in our minds in the pursuit of everyday life – apart from the politicians, of course, who seemed to have buried their heads in the sand, like the ostrich, hoping that the problems would go away. That is how it looked to me, anyway. Only Winston Churchill was agitating with his usual charismatic vigour and was warning of the danger that lay ahead for our country.

I was young and carefree and could probably have been forgiven for asking myself what the future held for me. I needed to do something positive. There was little doubt that the country would be at war with Germany in the not-too-distant future and I knew that I was of an age when I would be called up to serve my country. I convinced myself that I should do what I wanted to do, before being told what I had to do. The Territorial Army appealed to me so on the 24th day of April 1939 I made my way to Middlesbrough and enlisted in the 6th Battalion of the Green Howards. I had, for better or for worse, taken a step which would influence my life for many years and, at the time, I could not possibly have envisaged what traumatic events lay ahead of me.

I duly attended the weekly sessions at the drill hall in Lytton Street, Middlesbrough, and these culminated in my going to the annual training camp at Marton, near Morecambe. We were, of course, under canvas in bell tents, which were most uncomfortable – a taste of things to come. The weather was atrocious and the ground was a quagmire; we had to walk everywhere on duckboards.

Route marches were the order of the day and these were usually of twenty miles. The only weapon we had was a Lee Enfield rifle, which was a bolt-action, magazine-fed, repeating rifle. But we did not even attend a firing range in order to acquaint us with the weapon. I remember that the song of the day was 'South of the Border' and we gave it some stick on our marches.

It is almost unbelievable to me that the story I am now going to tell started on a lovely English summer's day in August 1939 – over fifty years ago – and would not end until almost six and a half years later. My twenties would have gone but on the credit side I would be a much travelled and wiser individual in every way. At that time I was on a camping holiday with three pals; our site was on lovely farmland at Crediton in Devon. I had never travelled so far south before and it had been my intention to go as far as Lands End. My car was a Morris Ten, registration VN 9248, and had been bought new for 187 pounds and 10 shillings – a lot of money then. It was a lovely warm sunny day, in an unspoilt meadow where wild flowers were growing in abundance, and the larks hovered in the sky. I hadn't a care in the world.

I had been for a dip in the river which ran at the bottom of the field, and on my way back called at the farm for fresh milk and eggs which we had for breakfast – life was wonderful. I stretched out on the grass, under a scorching sun, my head resting on my arms, thinking, and listening to the wireless. Around 10.30 am the programme was interrupted for a news flash and at that moment my little world fell apart.

The newsreader announced that a national emergency had been declared and that all members of the Territorial Army were to report to their headquarters without delay, to be ready for service in two days' time. I was flabbergasted; it was 22 August 1939 and a day I would never forget.

Our camping holiday came to an abrupt end and we all set to, pulling the tent down and packing the car. We were soon on our way back home up north, three hundred and twenty miles away. Those were the days when sixty mph was speeding; drivers were not as aggressive as they are today; they loved their cars and it was indeed a joy to drive; nobody was in a hurry to get from A to B.

One of the boys was named Don Savage, but more of him later in my story, which has a happy beginning and a happy ending, but a great number of events in between are tinged with sadness and sorrow.

What follows is the story of my twenties; there was no need to dream what I would do with my life, destiny had that all worked out for me.

Chapter 2

Call-up

I REPORTED to my unit, the 6th Green Howards (B Company), on 24 August 1939, the day before my 22nd birthday, and was not very impressed with the situation which greeted me. There were khaki-clad figures everywhere, doing nothing but rushing about trying to look important with no serious thought in mind, not knowing what a situation the country had got itself into. Young men of the Territorial Army kept arriving from all parts of the North Riding of Yorkshire – this was the catchment area from which the Green Howards regiment was formed.

The 6th Battalion, Green Howards, was part of an English county regiment, the 19th Foot of Alexandra, the Princess of Wales own Yorkshire Regiment, whose depot was at Richmond, Yorkshire. The regiment was first raised in 1688 by a Colonel Luttrell and had a great number of battle honours which would be upheld, and added to, in the Second World War. Being one of the few regiments left to retain its name, it formed a vital part of Her Majesty's Forces, serving anywhere trouble was found; it comprised good and true men and at the risk of me being pompous, splendid soldiers, as our record shows.

We went to the company stores and withdrew our rifles and bayonets plus whatever other kit was available, but it was very obvious that there was a great shortage of everything, though this was quite understandable and time would remedy that. It all went to prove how totally unprepared the country was for the emergency. One would have thought that the Munich crisis of 1938 (which involved Germany dismembering Czechoslovakia while the rest of Europe did nothing about it) would have set some alarm bells ringing in Government circles. They should at least have suspected that things had to come to a head and made an attempt at ensuring the forces were tuned up to a higher state of readiness than they were.

We were each issued with two blankets, which had to be signed for, as had every item of equipment we were issued with. At least, being a member of the Territorial Army gave us the privilege of having a genuine rifle rather than a wooden one, though up to that time we had not been given any practice with live ammunition – but the time would come.

I managed to secure a space away from the door, because of all the comings and goings. There were about fifty of us in the drill hall and it was bedlam – with everyone trying to talk at the same time, discussing where they were when they were called up. A few of us who were pals managed to be near each other.

The store man was Ray Dale; he was such a character, and I got on well with him. He was very serious and most conscientious as a store man and he used to think, or at least gave the impression, that we were all claiming something we were not entitled to, but he was really a good-hearted lad. He came from Bishop Auckland in County Durham. Two-by-four was like gold dust to him – this was a piece of thin flannel material that we used to clean the bore of our rifle with.

My first pal was a boy named Ivor Castor, who lived at Grangetown. He was a good, down-to-earth, northeast lad who had worked at the Dorman Long steel works, nearby, and was nineteen years of age and a very strong lad. As the war progressed he became bored with the routine of life in the infantry so volunteered for the paratroops and subsequently lost an arm when he was in action at Arnhem during the bungled Market Garden operation. I met him when I was on leave and his extrovert character had changed to introvert – his experiences had shattered his ego.

Another boy was Les Blowers, a likeable lad with a very quiet nature, but I eventually lost touch with him. Pals in the army were like shadows; they came and went with great frequency.

A few reservists had to be recalled and were distributed around different platoons. Naturally, they pretended they knew all there was to know about everything but actually didn't know a great deal at all. They were supposed to keep us young lads on the straight and narrow and bolster our morale. In fact we got the impression that they were only a pack of scroungers. We were young, healthy, high-spirited lads and we mucked in really well right from the start, whereas the ex-regulars were about thirty years of age and mostly married. They were not very reliable and gradually crawled their way into jobs where they felt sure they would not take part in any battles. In the course of time, most of these older men were not the soldiers who set an example when confronted by the enemy. There were exceptions, of course; genuine characters who really gave us their support.

For some months after call up I was stationed at Middlesbrough, Redcar, Stockton and Hartlepool, mainly doing guard duties. My first Sergeant Major was named Jerry O'Grady who obviously hailed from Ireland. He was about forty years of age and liked the sound of his own voice. He had a red face and bull neck and liked his drink; he was a bit of a bully and had his favourites, who also did their share of drinking.

The Regimental Sergeant Major was called Hughes and was a very strict disciplinarian but fair, which was a good thing. I recall he was only about five feet two inches in height and was very broad-shouldered. He looked very formidable to us young lads. I am sure he was almost as wide as he was tall – that is how I imagined him, anyway! He was, of course, a regular soldier and conveyed the impression that the whole conduct of the war depended on him – but that misapprehension had developed in him through his long association with discipline in the army. I can see him now and can hear his deep voice. He would bellow on the parade ground, which was at that time, a large grass field. He would shout, 'Prade-Prade-Chow!' which translated means 'Parade – attention!' Although he gave the impression that he was very bad-tempered, I always felt that it was an act of discipline, and this had to be enforced because if we understood the meaning of the word, we would make good soldiers. This tyrant was doing a thorough job and expected us to respond. It was the foundation of the British Army, which was second to none in the world. RSM Hughes gave us a very good grounding on how to behave ourselves and conduct ourselves with honour.

Our commanding officer was named Lieutenant Colonel Steel – an excellent, fair-minded soldier. Our B Company commander was Captain Chapman. About November 1939 we received two new Second Lieutenants. One was Hughes and the other was C. M. Hull, who proved over the years to be a very brave and popular officer who eventually attained the rank of Major. He was very conscientious from the start; I can see him now, he was only of small stature and he would step it out, cane under his left arm and when he returned a salute there was nothing half-hearted about it.

Most officers were of first-class material and considering they were not regular soldiers performed wonders with great enthusiasm, despite such meagre resources as were available at the time; therefore earning a well-deserved respect from their platoons, which responded with extra effort when called upon. They carried out their duties with utmost vigilance, an important part of which was learning how to understand and handle men of such different personalities. Just as in civilian life, men in uniform had their own peculiar characteristics, some quiet and reserved, others boisterous and aggressive – they resented the enforced discipline – yet when the time came for us to go into action, they were first-class soldiers.

Of course, there was always the man who showed signs of revolt. Consequently, he had to serve a period of punishment, which usually consisted of being put on a 252 (an army charge sheet), followed by seven days' 'jankers'. This meant that he was at the beck and call of the duty Non-Commanding Officer (NCO) – doing things like peeling sacks of spuds – which was an unenviable task and, of course, he was also confined to barracks or camp depending on our location.

It was my experience, many times, as the years passed, that these regular offenders made excellent soldiers – the most dependable in the face of adversity – and always gave of their best under active service conditions – they were afraid of nothing.

We did not have any weapons larger than a rifle so weapon training was out of the question. Nobody gave us any lectures about battle tactics in a given situation and no field training of any description was undertaken, partly because no up-to-date training manuals had been made available to us – our officers must have felt very frustrated. It seemed to me that the country found itself in a disastrous situation.

When I was called up my pay was two shillings (10p) a day and half of this was made into an allowance for my mother. This fifty-fifty arrangement continued throughout the war, as my pay increased. Pay in the army was a constant source of complaint among the lads and we were almost always broke. Comparing our rewards with American forces, we were paupers and as we fought the same war it was most unfair. As the saying goes – we just had to grin and bear it!

Pay Parade was an event not to be missed and it would be up on the company notice board what time pay would be given out. An officer would be at a table, with an army blanket spread out on it, and a clerk would be sitting at one end. A queue would form about six yards away and a soldier would step out smartly and salute, say his number and name, and hand his pay book to the clerk who would confirm this. He would then hold his hand out smartly to the officer, say, 'Thank you, sir!' salute, about turn and step it out. On active service this went by the board; we received pay if and when it was convenient.

Before the outbreak of war I ran a grocer's shop in conjunction with my mother, but our shop had now been closed down and our car sold; strange how I did not feel the loss of them. On the other hand, life in the army was a new adventure, and if one adapted to it, that was fine. I had before me a whole new way of life, and I never found any difficulty in coming to terms with it, even though there were complaints when we didn't know what was going on. We seemed to be going nowhere fast, during those early months of the war. Perhaps it was a good thing at the time that I did not realize what a most exciting, dangerous and traumatic, but rewarding, experience I had embarked upon. At times everybody became a little bored or 'browned-off' as we always said in the army, but one thing that kept most of us going was the comradeship which existed amongst lads who had been complete strangers such a short while ago. This esprit de corps would become embedded in our attitudes as time went by, and become invaluable when we went into battle when on many occasions our lives could depend upon our pals. Life in the army really was not so bad, once we had had our little moan amongst ourselves.

In no way at the present time was the Territorial Army on a par with the Regular Army. We were not equipped, mentally or physically, to take offensive action against a determined and well-armed enemy. It was going to take time for us to become what was expected of the British soldier and it would not happen overnight, though it most certainly would come about. Also, of course, the factories would require time to come on stream to produce the weapons of war we were all waiting for, and the labour force, too, needed time to adjust to the mainly repetitive work many of them would have to do.

I suppose the officers, particularly the younger ones who were keen and raring to go, were coming to grips with the responsibilities which had been thrust upon them, almost overnight getting to know men of very different characters and forming them into a cohesive force. Whereas a soldier knew what was expected of him and was loyal to his officers, young officers had to have the capacity to absorb tremendous quantities of knowledge; a platoon officer was responsible for the lives and welfare of thirty young men and this was no small undertaking.

I had now been in uniform for six months; the time seemed to have passed quickly and although our work up to now had been fairly humdrum and repetitive, there was no doubt about it, we were fitter than we were six months ago and this had been achieved without any undue effort.

Six months after the outbreak of war, we had still not received any additional weapons and a great deal of our time seemed to be wasted. It is almost unbelievable that for eight months from call-up all we did were drill parades, guard duties on the coast, kit inspection and the usual non-productive activities – we had not even talked about any kind of tactics, or even undertaken a route march to toughen us up. Not a finger was lifted to train us for war. It seemed that everybody thought that if our Army kept quiet Hitler would go away.

So, during April 1940, we went to France, not to fight the Germans but to construct an airstrip!

Chapter 3

We Join the British Expeditionary Force (BEF)

DURING THE third week of March 1940 we were all given seven days' embarkation leave. Of course, there was only one destination for us – the British Expeditionary Force, consisting of regular soldiers, was already in France preparing for the time when the Germans decided to make a move.

The beginning of April found us marching to Stockton-on-Tees railway station where our special train awaited us. As soon as the train started to move, the playing cards were produced and the mouth organs came out. Those were very carefree days and our problems and anxieties were in the future – who cared about tomorrow? A good thing we did not know what tomorrow might bring!

The journey to Dover was uneventful and we were soon walking up the gangplank to board the ship which was bound for Calais. For most of us it would be the first time we had been outside of England so that whatever happened from now on would be a new experience. The sea was kind to us first-timers and nobody was seasick. When stepping ashore, we could hardly believe what we were seeing – marching, or rather slouching, along the quayside was a motley gathering; it seemed to have been left behind from the First World War. A continuous procession of French soldiers walked aimlessly along the quayside accompanied by hundreds of horses, some pulling antiquated artillery pieces; there was no mechanical transport of any kind. They were ambling along as though next week would do, and were followed by officers in uniform on horseback. Well, if these were our allies, the war would soon be over, LOST. There was a total lack of discipline and, with hindsight, that must be one of the reasons for the French collapse when confronted by such a formidable enemy. An efficient army must have discipline and be able to carry out orders without question.

We entrained on the dockside and journeyed to a place called Irles, from where we marched five miles into the French countryside, and were billeted in farm barns where we bedded down on clean straw. Conditions were very primitive – no hot and cold here, or electric light. We washed and shaved in a stream, which ran along the bottom of the field, and the weather was bitterly cold into the bargain. We had received a rude awakening – so this was France.

We, B Company, were now part of the 23rd Division, Territorial Army and, together with the 7th Green Howards and the 5th East Yorks, formed the 69th

Brigade of that division. There were three battalions in a brigade and three brigades in a division. The 69th had a future which would be outstanding in the British Army, but at present it was the intention of the War Office that we were in France not to confront the enemy but to prepare landing strips for the Royal Air Force, since we were not yet in any way equipped for battle.

For three weeks we worked very hard, and practically lived in our overalls, or denims as they were called. It is strange how certain things stick in one's memory, but whenever we stayed in one place for longer than a day, the first thing to be done was the provision of latrines. Here, the latrine took the form of a deep trench about eighteen inches wide and a long pole was suspended lengthways above the trench – use your imagination about the end of that little saga! Like it or lump it, whatever the weather, that was what soldiers called the bog! Compared to the conditions of those far off days, today's soldiers are living in paradise.

Whilst we were levelling the land, many 1914–18 war relics, including still-lethal mortar bombs, were unearthed. We also had our first sighting of German aircraft, which bombed and strafed us, causing some casualties.

Fifth column activities were reported to be on the increase with the result that regular patrols were sent out during the night, looking for saboteurs. One of these patrols discovered two men shining torches into the sky when aircraft were overhead. They were taken into custody and handed over to the French police who just took them away and shot them.

We were always kept in the dark and just obeyed orders from day-to-day, so did not know how the war was going. But we did know that suddenly we stopped work on the runway and were given our marching orders. It was 10 May 1940 and at last the real war had started; the Germans were calling the tune by invading Holland and Belgium.

We quickly marched to a place called Saucy Caudry, where we proceeded to dig slit trenches for the first time, the first of many, taking up defensive positions with our rifles; this left us in no doubt that our real part in the war was beginning to materialize.

Bear in mind we were not equipped to do battle, apart from our rifles, which none of us had yet fired. Also, each company, A, B, C, D and Headquarters Company (each about 100 men) had two Bren guns and one anti-tank rifle and this was fired from the ground, against the shoulders, which it was said was put out of joint by the recoil of the rifle. As yet, nobody had fired any of these weapons. We had no Bren carriers or mortars and almost no signal equipment and no divisional artillery. Our officers did not have a revolver, binoculars or compass unless they had brought their own from England. And here we were, waiting for the blitzkrieg. It was unbelievable that such a situation had been allowed to develop, knowing that Germany had been preparing for war for years. To think that we were expected to repulse an enemy attack on our front; it was ludicrous, but that was the situation in which we found ourselves. I can only suppose that the enemy were not aware of our predicament or we would have been overrun in no time.

It had been intended that we should return to England after three months to complete our training. However, within a few weeks, though many of us had hardly fired a rifle, we found ourselves fighting for our lives and holding up the onrushing Germans like seasoned warriors.

On 17 May, our 6th Battalion took up positions along the Canal Du Nord, a front of seventeen miles, and as we had not been supplied with any other weapons with which to carry out this formidable task, it was farcical. Fortunately, we were not put under any real pressure here.

At this time, the Sergeant Major came up to me and asked how I fancied being batman and runner to the company commander, Major Petch. I was more than a little browned off with the unsoldierly work I was doing so, for better or worse, I said yes. Looking back to those days, that step changed my whole army career, and at least the job was interesting and introduced me to a different way of life, and how officers did, or did not do, their duty over the years. I could have refused to be batman in which case I knew that promotion would come anyway, but I am sure I made the right decision. Major Petch was a good, kindly man and I enjoyed attending to his needs. He was a gentleman farmer in civilian life and Clerk of Redcar Racecourse. He adored his B Company and looking after him gave me much pleasure. He would say, 'Now then, Cheall – I am doing so-and-so today. I will need you to accompany me'. It was good while it lasted. He really was a gentleman and never forgot that the lads were human beings as well as soldiers.

On 18 May, rumours were received that enemy tanks had entered Cambrai, as a result of which one of our officers had to blow up a bridge to deny its use to the enemy. This was done in spite of the fact that refugees refused to stop crossing while the bridge was blown. The result was dreadful and many civilians were killed and maimed. It was the first of many horrific scenes we would witness.

We were like pieces on a chessboard and were constantly on the move. Next day we were withdrawn to Saudemont and took up new defensive positions. It was open country and difficult to defend because it was ideal for tanks to operate. The enemy would know our every move, because there was never-ending activity from their spotter planes and we were bombed regularly. It really was very daunting to be in the situation in which we found ourselves but until we were more adequately armed, what could we do with our rifles? Fortunately, up to now, we had not been confronted by enemy tanks, only infantry, and were able to repulse any attacks they made. Now, to make conditions worse, we were given notice that rations were to be reduced by half because supplies were not getting through in sufficient quantities. In fact, no further normal issue of rations reached us for the next fifteen days – we certainly felt the effect of this because after all we were fit, young men and we all had a moan even though nobody could do anything about it – we just made the best of a bad situation. Supplies of every kind were being affected by the total lack of preparedness for war and the soldiers were having to pay the price of the politicians' shortsightedness.

Two days later, I had to take a message from Major Petch to Battalion HQ. Because of the lack of signal equipment, I had to use the company motorcycle as the companies were dispersed. Travelling along the roads was a bit hazardous because of bomb craters, plus enemy shells were exploding in the fields around, together with the fact that we never knew from day-to-day where the enemy would turn up. Suddenly, I came across an ambulance which had crashed into a hedgerow. I approached carefully, only to discover that it had been abandoned after being hit by a shell. Not being able to resist the temptation, I had a cautious look in the back to discover not bodies, for which I was pleased, but instead, lo and behold, a full case of Heinz baked beans; I was over the moon! I could hardly believe my luck. Putting the box across the petrol tank I delivered the message to HQ where no end of persuasion would relieve me of my find. I returned to my company where the lads were overjoyed and the look of delight on the cooks' faces was great. We crushed up some of our hard tack biscuits and mixed them into the beans in a Dixie for a feast indeed! It was smashing even though it had to be eaten cold, as no fires were allowed in our present position.

On 22 May, we were ordered to take up new positions on the bank of the River Scarpe at Roeux. The move was made during the hours of darkness and we had to dig in before dawn, feeling very hungry and tired, but everything had to be done with great urgency. No news was coming through to us, though it was obvious that feverish activity was going on in the chain of command. The front was changing so swiftly that it now came as tragic news to us that the Germans had broken the line, with the result that our 70th Brigade had met with disaster. Tanks had overrun them and many of the lads had been killed or captured.

This was a dreadful blow to us and it could so easily have been our own brigade which had suffered that fate. The enemy facing us were just across the river and were putting down mortar fire so we had to retreat yet again to Farbus and while we were dug in at this position, more weapons were given to us. Each section of ten men now had a Bren gun – which none of us had as yet had the opportunity to fire on a range in England. Each platoon had a two-inch mortar; also an anti-tank rifle, which was capable of knocking out a light enemy tank, so we now felt able to put up a better resistance than was previously the case, and we certainly felt able to repulse at least an attack by infantry.

We were now no longer a labour battalion. A few more weapons had been brought up to us so we were now an active service unit and were continually on the move as the enemy in front of us became more menacing and the Territorial soldiers were replaced by more seasoned troops who were properly trained.

Each time we were forced to withdraw we experienced yet another tragedy. During the march to Farbus – along the country roads, so that enemy aircraft would not so easily observe our movement – we had to mix with the refugees who crowded the roads everywhere. That was an experience I will remember as long as I live. Old men, women and children pushing anything on wheels – bicycles, prams, barrows, handcarts – anything to save carrying more than they had to. Then there were the poor horses, pulling over-laden carts. The families had brought with them as many of their possessions as they possibly could. It must have been heartbreaking to leave their homes, possibly for the last time, knowing full well that the enemy would loot them.

Very suddenly, the sound of aircraft would be heard and everybody looked fearfully to the sky. Out of that beautiful blue sky would come death and destruction. The planes made a beeline for the poor folk, dropping their lethal loads, zooming into the sky and then flying the length of the refugee column machine-gunning anything and everything – it was horrifying. Absolute chaos was created among that pathetic humanity; dead bodies and parts of bodies lay everywhere. Children scared to death, not being able to understand, lying across dead mothers, many of whom had their intestines oozing from their stomachs. Horses were going mad and dragging bits of the carts over the bodies spread all across the road.

I recall watching an old man and woman who, upon seeing the bullets making a path along the road, put their arms around each other and they both fell dead. I cannot say any more because it is impossible for words to describe the events clearly enough for anybody to understand – it had to be seen to be believed. By the time it was dusk we found ourselves making our weary way to our next position and we were harassed all the way to the wooded slopes of Vimy Ridge of First World War fame. Many of the lads thought about how their fathers could so easily have fought and died on these same wooded slopes fighting Germans in that war. Our experience was that we were fighting a callous and ruthless German Army – fanatical – and armed with vastly superior weaponry to our own. We were there merely to make the numbers up, not being in a position to be aggressive because we had not sufficient effective weapons to cause the enemy any concern; we were therefore always on the defensive.

It was impossible for us to remain on Vimy Ridge. We were shelled, bombed and mortared, and because of our casualties, which we could ill-afford, we had to retire once again, but we did our utmost for two days. None of us had slept properly or washed for days and we were very tired and hungry, but most of us were still alive. On the third day we marched, again, to a position near Roclincourt and dug in.

During all the time we spent in England, we hadn't done one route march to prepare us and toughen us up. As far as my feet were concerned, I was lucky I didn't have any trouble, but many of the lads were having it rough with blisters, and food was very short also. Our 23rd Division was now placed under the command of General Headquarters in order that we could play our part in the defence of the perimeter, which was becoming more compressed as each day passed.

Quite unexpectedly (but necessary, because of the distance involved) a convoy of three-tonners (which is how we described army three-ton lorries) turned up to transport us. We hastily enbussed because we were required to plug a hole in another part of the front. During the journey the enemy paid us some attention and two of our trucks were forced off the road and overturned. We were gradually accumulating more weapons, many of them found lying on the roadside.

On the journey we passed through Arras. The whole town was a mass of flames after repeated enemy bombing and it was a risk driving through the place because of the danger of falling brickwork and timbers. We travelled about seventy miles to Gravelines, which is on the coast ten miles east of Calais, which was almost – at this stage – surrounded on three sides and there was a tremendous battle raging there. Calais, where it all began for us in April. It seemed ages ago and we felt as though we had not slept or eaten since then. So much had happened that time was no longer of any consequence. Our company commander, Major Petch, was a tower of strength to us all and I could almost feel him suffering inwardly for the safety of his lads.

During the journey of 23rd Division, the Germans attacked and the road was out, so only we 6th Green Howards got through to Gravelines. Again, the priority was to dig ourselves slit trenches, an art at which we were becoming very adept. Together with some French, we dug defensive positions. Our position ran along the bank of the River Aa. It had taken us all night, without sleep, and dawn of 23 May was on the horizon when our positions were ready. Despite the situation in which we found ourselves, it was remarkable that the lads were not downhearted in any way, and if it came to a showdown the enemy would pay dearly for his adventure into our area; it says a great deal about the characters and tenacity of our lads. The only problem as far as we were concerned at that time was food! Again, it was almost impossible to sleep; the bombing was on a regular basis. Some of the lads were killed while they slept through exhaustion, and for the first time for days we had our first hot meal – bully (corned beef) stew and hard tack biscuits to break into it, and it gave us new heart.

Our battalion had an excellent commanding officer in Lieutenant Colonel Steel who was very understanding and considerate since we were experiencing such adverse conditions – having been upgraded from a labour battalion to an active service role in such a short time must have put a dreadful strain on all our officers. The enemy made a probing attack against us with light tanks and infantry and we succeeded in knocking out one tank and scattering the infantry. During the afternoon, three light tanks were seen approaching our positions; the black cross was clearly visible. None of us had been given the responsibility of the Boyes anti-tank rifle, which was suspected of having terrific recoil. This situation, of course, like many other situations we experienced, was the result of our lack of training in England. One of our young officers, Second Lieutenant Hewson, took it upon himself to attack the enemy. He succeeded in knocking out one of the tanks, but the flash from the anti-tank rifle gave his position away and as he was endeavouring to change his position he was fired upon by the enemy and killed. The German infantry who accompanied the tanks made a show of making an attack upon us and we retaliated aggressively, killing many of them and causing them to withdraw. We were so incensed over the death of our brave young officer! We recovered Second Lieutenant Hewson's body the next day and he is buried at Fort-Mardyck near Dunkirk.

During the early hours of the next morning, we were defending a bridge at Gravelines when four tanks approached us from the direction of Calais and we fired upon them causing them to withdraw out of sight. Very soon afterwards, the same tanks came towards us yet again, but this time flying red white and blue streamers and they turned out to be British tanks which had been cut off during a tank battle outside of Calais – they immediately joined us in the defence of Gravelines.

We lost some good lads here because apart from the bombing by the Stukas, we were being shelled by the 88mm guns. The enemy infantry tried yet again to attack us, causing casualties to both sides and, not realizing how near we were to the enemy, some of our other ranks were taken prisoner, as were Captain Kidd, Captain Foster and Second Lieutenant Farrand, the latter being already wounded. All the inhabitants must either have fled or were hiding in cellars because we didn't see a single civilian.

Considering our strength, we had put up a good show against a very forceful enemy who knew that he had the upper hand and that it was only a matter of time before their victory was assured.

For the action we fought at Gravelines, several officers received decorations including our Lieutenant Colonel Steel who received a bar to his DSO and we were mentioned by name in the despatches of Lord Gort.

Chapter 4

Dunkirk

OUR POSITION, because of our dwindling strength and lack of support was in some peril and we were in grave danger of being cut off from other British forces, when orders came through for us to abandon our positions and march to Bergues, to join in the defence of the perimeter of Dunkirk, alongside more experienced soldiers, namely the Welsh Guards and Irish Guards. The enemy artillery and mortars paid us plenty of attention and, again, we lost some good lads.

However, our orders to march to Bergues were no sooner given than they were countermanded, with the result that we had to move into the line at Haeghe Meulen, protecting the right flank of the main axis of withdrawal to Dunkirk.

Considering the losses we had suffered and the lack of good training during the early months and given that we were now fighting alongside seasoned soldiers, our grit, determination and morale were excellent – even though the problems of hunger and lack of sound sleep were ever present. It says a great deal about the leadership of our officers and the fighting spirit of the lads.

It was a huge consolation to us that we were now better armed, particularly with the very important Bren guns and anti-tank rifles. Also, plenty of ammunition had been accumulated because our lads were constantly retrieving it, along with the weapons, from the roadside. They had been thrown away by irresponsible soldiers who had previously passed through in their haste to reach Dunkirk as lightly laden and as quickly as possible. Those weapons should have been brought back to England for use in the future. Probably, the lads who discarded their weapons had come to the conclusion that considering their predicament, the war was lost because nothing seemed to be going right.

We had no illusions about our capabilities and we knew that there was a great deal to be done about our potential, both mentally and physically, before we would be able to resist for long such a powerful and well-prepared enemy as we now faced. But we were determined to give as good as we got within the limits of our capabilities. We knew that we could not take any aggressive action but felt able to give a damned good account of ourselves and show the Jerries that we were not going to be a walkover.

Our officers had to guide us out of this nightmarish debacle and leave the stubborn defence of the perimeter to the more experienced and older soldiers who, had they been in possession of sufficient weapons, would not have let the enemy pass. With the weaponry they had, the rearguard at Dunkirk did a tremendous job of containing the enemy whilst the bulk of the BEF escaped to fight another day.

Morale was good after our brush with the enemy at Gravelines and we felt confident that we could put up a sound defence - good north-country lads were not going to be disposed of so easily, even though the enemy had far superior fire power, but we did lose some good boys at this time. After all is said and done, only three weeks ago most of us had not even fired a rifle, and now here we were, acting as last line of defence in our sector.

By this time we were becoming very tired, as sleep had been impossible for some nights – hunger and blistered feet also took their toll and the enemy pressure had been relentless. I could not remember the last time we had had our boots off, changed our socks or had a wash. All our kit had been lost in the transport, but our officers were magnificent and urged us on in a bid to reach the coast. The NCOs, too, were stouthearted men. Pep talks by our officers worked wonders with morale. After one of these talks our Sergeant came amongst us and said: 'Right, lads, who wants a shower?' The immediate response was 'Bugger off, Sarg!' It only took a bit of a joke and morale was back to normal. They were a grand lot of lads in the army. I think what the lads missed most was a good cigarette, in fact any cigarette would have done! I was lucky in that respect because I had never smoked and was never tempted to, so I could not understand their craving.

During the period of Dunkirk, we were never demoralised and had faith in our officers to see us through. To a very large extent we were all in the dark about what was going on, until it became clear to us that gradually we were making our way to the beaches. Each order to move took us closer and it became obvious that many of us would be killed or captured, and right now we felt very tired, hungry and dirty.

Comradeship was at a premium and its values had surfaced on many occasions during the past weeks. Our company commander, Major Leslie Petch, amazed me. I was still batman and runner and I risked my life many times taking messages to the other companies, but more often to Battalion HQ. I, more than anybody else in the company, saw the personal side of him. He was a brick and a tower of strength, setting an example to every one of us by his stoical character – more so since he was quite a bit overweight, but he was overflowing with determination and always retained his gentlemanly attitude.

Many times I saw him sitting on a wall or rock, or just sitting on the ground, staring and thinking, giving me the impression that he was silently praying for his lads. I would say, 'I'll go and see if I can scrounge a mess tin of tea, shall I, sir?' Wherever we halted there was always some lad whose first thought was a brew, and somehow he always managed it. His reply would always be, 'That would be grand, Cheall, but you must not take any risks, we can all have as much tea as we want when we get back to England, and we will get back, God is watching over us.' He really was a true English gentleman.

After two days of beating off attempted infiltrations by the enemy infantry and killing many of them, the order came (during the evening of 29 May) for us to retire further towards the coast at Dunkirk – a distance of about ten miles. The Regular Army battalion of the Welsh guards was taking over our sector and we had to hand over all weapons, except for our rifles. The Guards, unlike the Territorials, were fully trained soldiers; they had undergone intensive training and all were a year or two older than us Territorial Army men. They had their splendid traditions to uphold and would give any aggressive intent by the enemy short shrift – until they became exhausted or ran short of ammunition.

Our perimeter was being squeezed ever smaller and the front had to be manned so far as was possible by seasoned troops. Each division had a section of the coast to reach in order to try and get on a boat. But before the battalion could extricate itself a tragedy occurred. The enemy broke through the Welsh Guards and our D Company. Many men of one platoon (about thirty men) were killed and run over by German tanks, only four escaping.

The evacuation beaches covered a length of coastline running from La Panne to Dunkirk. The sector we were heading for was in between at a place called Bray-Dunes, which was about central and must have derived its name from the sand dunes which ran off the beach. Our path lay across open countryside and this kept us away from the roads which were still crowded with the hapless refugees who were being forced to the side by an endless convoy of all kinds of military vehicles, pushing their way forward in order to get as close as possible to the beaches. I thought our officers were brilliant in guiding us through that nightmarish countryside.

We looked a very sorry sight, covered in dirt and grime, with hunger gnawing at our bellies – I now weighed only ten stones, having lost seven pounds from the time I left England only eight weeks ago; this of course was confirmed when I returned to England.

Our aircraft were significant by their absence, but we discovered the reason for this later; the Royal Air Force had been about as prepared for war as the army. I am sure that despite the meagre resources available to them, the RAF performed well in other parts of the battlefront unseen by us. They were young men, just like us, and could not perform miracles. The politicians had a great deal to answer for by ignoring the continuous signs of the German preparation for conflict.

Difficult as it was, ploughing across farmland with the mud coming above our boots and still being strafed by machine guns from the planes, we must have made better time than those using the roads, because a few miles from the beaches a massive graveyard started. Many thousands of vehicles had been driven as far as they could get towards Dunkirk, then made useless and abandoned or set on fire. It really is impossible for me to describe the havoc which had been created. Both ways, as far as we could see, the vehicles had been set ablaze, as were petrol and ammunition dumps spreading smoke and flames over a wide area – but it would deny the enemy the use of it. The cost must have been tremendous.

It was some miles to Bray-Dunes. In the distance a huge column of thick black smoke reached for the sky – the oil tanks at Dunkirk were ablaze.

I will never forget the sad necessity of so much destruction or the sight of dead soldiers and civilians lying all over the place. Nobody had time to bury them and our medics were already doing more than could really be expected of them, taking care of the wounded. Then there were the cattle – the poor helpless animals running madly about, scared out of their wits, the dead ones lying on their backs, legs in the air and bloated like balloons. And there were packs of scavenging dogs, almost wild, driven mad by the effects of the bombing.

There was no panic; at least I did not see any sign of it. The army just had to make haste to the beaches and we had to try and keep with our own unit. If anybody became separated from his company, it would not have been a very pleasant experience, but as time passed this is what happened to some of the lads.

In the background we could hear the cacophony of war, where the British Army and the best of the French soldiers were giving their all in a desperate bid to hold the enemy back so that as many of the army as possible could reach the evacuation beaches and get away before the inevitable happened. Many of the rear guards would be overrun by an invincible force, to be taken prisoner to face a most uncertain period of time at the mercy of the enemy, not knowing how long it would be before they saw their loved ones again.

It was just as well that the folk at home could not possibly have any idea what their men folk were enduring or they would most certainly have thought that the war was already lost. As for the soldiers themselves, they were there, as it happened, not knowing what fate had in store for them. It was a most dreadful period in our lives; who could say what the end of all this trauma would be? I do not know where the war correspondents were in those days, or even if the force had any photographers, but in retrospect it seems to me that not much coverage of the British in action is available; that was a most deplorable oversight.

We still had our rifles, small packs and water bottles – our large packs having been lost as they would have gone astray with the company stores with the divisional transport. The enemy must have had a whale of a time sorting out the captured material when the evacuation ended. We had no other weapons apart from one Bren gun and this weapon was not going to fall into German hands! Mind you, a Bren weighs almost twenty-three pounds [just over three gallons of milk – Ed] and a 303 Enfield rifle weighed eight and a half pounds. The Bren gunner and his mate loved that weapon, taking turns to carry it and despite all the mud and filth we had gone through, it was spotlessly clean. Those two grand lads eventually brought it back to England and there was almost a court martial about it. All weapons brought back from Dunkirk were supposed to be handed in and then redistributed at a later date. However, the Bren gunner was adamant that the weapon should remain with his platoon. Eventually, a higher-ranking officer agreed with his sentiments and the lad was almost overcome with emotion. Yes – soldiers do at times show emotion – and that illustrated how a very brave kid loved that weapon.

So, we had found our destination, Bray-Dunes, and had made our way to the East Mole at Dunkirk. Here I was on the evacuation ship, watching my destiny unfurl before me. I awoke from my memory rewind as the Stuka's bombs dropped in deadly silence towards us.

I saw the bombs leaving one of the planes and was certain our time had come, and that this was the end. I closed my eyes and gritted my teeth, my whole body braced for the inevitable impact. Then, 'Sploosh!' and nothing else. I looked out in surprised relief to find that, miraculously, the bombs had hit the sea about twenty yards away, so God was watching over us. Then we all gave a massive cheer when one of our destroyers hit one of the planes, knocking a wing off with the inevitable result.

As we drew away from the coast on 31 May 1940, I wondered how many of the soldiers left on the beach would get away. That night and all I saw will always be imprinted upon my memory.

After another mile or so we felt safer; we were going to be lucky. Everybody became so quiet that only the passage of the ship could be heard, and that noise was bliss to our ears. I don't believe that anybody who had endured the past weeks, witnessed such tragic events and lived to remember it all could be anything but thankful – there must be a God above looking after us. Even the least religious had been transformed into believers. I knew many lads who had tough characters and didn't give a damn for anything or anybody, but they closed their eyes as soon as the Padre said, 'Men, let us pray' – there were no objectors. God answered our prayers and gave us a safe passage back to our lovely country. I remember that during the journey to England most of us had snatches of sleep by just supporting each other; we were so exhausted by the lack of sleep, that nothing could keep us awake. Early morning, after it had become light, somebody shouted, 'Hey, look across there!' We saw the White Cliffs of Dover, and it was a beautiful sight. In a little while, the ship slowed down and soon edged its way to the dockside at Folkestone.

There was a tremendous welcome from everybody awaiting our arrival. Those good Samaritans of The Salvation Army and of the Women's Voluntary Service made us most welcome and plied us with sandwiches and mugs of good strong tea, and before we had time to gather our wits we were boarding trains. It was unbelievable that we had escaped from Dunkirk. So many good lads, the fighting rearguard in particular, would have to surrender and spend the remainder of the war in prison.

In no time at all we entrained for an unknown destination, but who cared; the English countryside looked magnificent and we were all very soon fast asleep.

It felt good to be alive. We only had our rifles, as we'd had to dump all other kit and we were dirty, tired, hungry and all bewildered, but we were home. God had answered our prayers and given us a safe passage back to England – beautiful England. We came back from France very much wiser and much more experienced than when we went eight weeks ago – only eight weeks but it seemed much longer. What an experience we had undergone, but the main thing was that we had lived to tell the tale and memories had been created which most of us young lads would never forget – the victorious withdrawal which snatched well over 300,000 men off the beaches to fight another day; young men, crying through shell shock, unable to control their feelings; seeing our pals alive one second, dead the next; all those small boats, getting as close to the shore as they could to pick up a few lads; the ship which had been sunk in the harbour, with funnels and superstructure showing above the water; seeing Arras one mass of flames. Nobody who has seen such horror and destruction can fail to wonder how we got into this predicament.

I believe the miracle of Dunkirk had a far wider significance than anybody imagined at the time. Most of the soldiers who came back were the youth of Britain end eventually formed the nucleus of the Eighth Army in Africa and the Fourteenth Army in Burma. The war could have lasted another two years had we not been brought back from Dunkirk.

Chapter 5

The Aftermath

WE HAD no sooner entrained than we were fast asleep. After about an hour, the whistle of the train awakened us all with a jolt. We soon pulled into a station and all piled out, bleary eyed, to be given as much tea and sandwiches as we wanted, but remember, it had been weeks since we had received a good meal and it came as a shock to realize we could only eat so much.

On our way again and there was plenty of time for reflection and recrimination about the course of what we had been through during the few short weeks since we had left England in high spirits in early April, supposedly to prepare landing strips for non-existent aeroplanes. Was it really only two months ago?

Probably on the credit side was the fact that what we had experienced would be something to think about, and be the topic of conversation, for many years to come. What a remarkable thing the human brain is, the amount of knowledge it can absorb; what about our eyes? What they have seen will never be forgotten – the poor haggard refugees who consisted of women, children and old folk, many of whom had lost all they held most dear, including their husbands. The helpless animals, scared out of their wits by the noises of war. The crowded beaches and those young soldiers who had lost their reason. That thick black smoke from the oil tanks reaching for the heavens. All those thousands of abandoned vehicles. The many ships which had been sunk in the water at Dunkirk, in their effort to get the lads away. There was also time to think about our salvation, because even though Dunkirk was a kind of defeat, in retrospect it was also a victory, in the sense that we had foiled the German attempt to create a catastrophe for England, also that the enemy now knew that the British soldier was a first-class fighter and that England was not going to be the same walkover as the continental countries had been.

Because of the stops we had to make, it took us about six hours to reach our destination, which was Cardiff. We detrained, again being made most welcome by the people on the platform. On the road, outside of the station, was a fleet of coaches (strange, we didn't march) which took us to a hutted camp about five miles from the city. There would be about twenty lads to a hut and each of us had a metal-framed bed, with three biscuits (thin mattresses), three feet by two feet on each bed. The biscuits were three inches thick and made a good bed; we also had three grey army blankets each.

We soon settled in because the only kit we had was the webbing equipment we wore, our small pack, steel helmet and, of course, our rifle. Oh, and I had brought my bayonet back from Dunkirk, not many of the lads had done so. Many years later, I gave it to the Green Howards museum in Richmond. On the beaches, many regiments had become mixed up with each other so the returning men were sent to various camps and sorted out. We were at Cardiff for that reason, to be sorted out and sent to our own regiments. I was lucky, as most of our boys had stuck together. We did not have any kit so had to wait until the full regalia of a soldier's kit was available, so we remained rather scruffy and unkempt.

An officer came round the huts, taking our names and checking identity discs and, of course, our requirements; it was not impossible for an infiltrator to have taken the opportunity to come over with us from Dunkirk. Right now, all different regiments were mixed together, just as we had been on the ships and the train, none of our officers were with us and there were only about fifty Green Howards.

After the checking had been completed, we fell in and marched to the dining hall where we had our first hot meal. There is no food to compare with good army grub, and it went down a treat. We had nothing to do at this camp; just laze around and rest our weary bodies. I lost no time in writing a few letters to my mother and friends to let them know that I was safe and well; letters they must have been very pleased to receive. All our families would have known that we had been in the debacle at Dunkirk and they must have been dreadfully worried, fearing the worst.

Two days passed, during which time we had been paid two pounds each from any pay that had accumulated to our credit. Then we were allowed out of camp, even though we only had the clothes we stood up in – everything else had been lost with the company stores.

The days passed, during which time we had done our best to clean ourselves up so that we were more presentable. We had no polish for our boots and our battle dress looked the worse for wear, but our first hot shower had been a treat, the first for weeks.

Although we were a bit bedraggled, permission was given to go into the city. I was sure the civilians would understand why we were not our usual smart selves. Under normal circumstances we would never have been allowed past the guardroom. As a rule, when soldiers left camp on leisure activities, there were always three or four together; it was more fun. However, this time it was different; I went out on my own. I was still wearing my steel helmet as I didn't have a cap, and we weren't allowed to go out bare head. I was the subject of scrutiny by the local populace, but they would know that I had been at Dunkirk and were doubtless thinking what a story I could tell, because they could not possibly have imagined what had been going on over there, but how could they? The truth was beyond imagination.

I had never been to Cardiff or to Wales for that matter, but even then didn't really have the time or inclination to look around. The army environment was not the most conducive way of life to make us want to explore the various places we were billeted at. Probably the main cause of this was that we were always very short of money.

I was feeling rather low as I stood reading a newssheet, which had been posted outside a newspaper office, when I had a very pleasant surprise. Two ladies came up to me; they would perhaps be in their early fifties and were well dressed, very pleasant and self-assured as they approached me. Although it was very obvious that I was one of the Dunkirk boys – well, I was only twenty-two – they put the question to me, and when I confirmed that I was, their faces lit up. They then asked me if I would do the honour of letting them take me to their homes for afternoon tea. I jumped at the opportunity and cordially accepted without further ado, thanking them. My first experience of the Welsh gave me a good feeling.

The ladies' names were Mrs Owens and Mrs Jones, two good Welsh names; they were both widows. They were all extremely middle-class people and lived in a lovely village called Fairwater, which was on the outskirts of Cardiff. Mrs Owens, who looked the elder, was rather keen to take me to her house first. She lived alone in an immaculate semi-detached house on Bwlch Road. After the three of us had had sandwiches and home-made cakes, we just sat and they told me about their own circumstances, how the war was affecting them and so on; they never mentioned Dunkirk, being such very kind, understanding and sympathetic souls. I was never to forget them or the way in which I had met them. To think that those two complete strangers had taken me under their wing and been so generous towards me; I was deeply affected. It was now time for me to be getting back to camp but, before I left, both ladies trying to speak at the same time asked me if I had any money. After telling them that I had just been paid, and thanking them profusely, Mrs Jones asked me if I could possibly get out of camp the next day and go to her house to have dinner with her and her sister Alice, also her brother-in-law, Roy. They both lived with Mrs Jones.

I did not have any problem about leaving camp next day so back I went to Fairwater. What a lovely name, and the three of them could not do enough for me, and I have had a deep regard for the Welsh ever since. They dined me as if I was one of their own. I was made so much at ease by their generosity, and I knew that they must be curious about Dunkirk so I told them of my experience in France. They just sat on the settee, spellbound, during which time the ladies, including Mrs Owens who had been invited, being the devout Christians they were, broke down and wept silently when I told them about the refugees. After I had told them what I knew they had been waiting to hear – and they had been absorbed, without interruption – they all gave me a most welcome hug and a kiss. It made me feel great.

All my six-and-a-half years in the army did not change my character and principles. I always minded my own business, had my pals and got on with the job.

Over the years that followed, I kept in touch with Mrs Jones, particularly, and spent two most enjoyable weekends at her house. All the family were so very kind to me. It was Margaret Jones who sent me a Methodist hymn book (now in my souvenir box) when I was billeted in Southwold some years later and the book is a treasured memory of days long past. It was very sad when I had to take my leave.

Dunkirk was now in the past, and we were much wiser men; the experience had taught us lads a great deal, and consequently we were much more capable soldiers, having endured an ordeal impossible within normal training schedules, and survived, all for two shillings a day. But with hindsight, under the circumstances, money was of little importance and that was a fair sum to pay us for the experience we had gained and the knowledge we young lads had accumulated under war conditions. It would be invaluable to us in time to come wherever the call of war took us, and we were destined to do quite a bit of travelling. I now knew what being an infantryman was all about.

Chapter 6

We Reorganize

WE WERE at Cardiff for about two and a half weeks, having been somewhat molly-coddled, fed very well and catching up on our sleep. Also, the boys who had suffered with blistered feet had been attended to. We had done enough lazing about and were now in danger of becoming bored and we needed to be on the move again.

There were lads here from many other regiments and having now been sorted out, the time had come for us to rejoin our own battalions, wherever they may have ended up. A fleet of three-tonners was lined up on the road through the camp, and the Green Howards filled three of them; there would be about forty-eight of us plus a Sergeant, and away we went. We ended up at Launceston in Cornwall; it was about 18 June and a lovely summer's day.

Quickly, things started to get moving; it was a Nissen-hutted camp, the first time we had come across this type of accommodation and it would most certainly not be the last. First thing to be done was a roll call to see who had survived, and therefore who was missing; it could have been a golden opportunity for anybody who felt the urge to desert. Now kit was issued to replace that which had been lost with the transport in France. Within days, the companies were made up to strength to replace the unfortunate boys who had been killed or taken prisoner; the new soldiers, most of whom were about nineteen years of age, had been sent from the regimental depot at Richmond, Yorkshire. It was good to be back in my old B Company, to be able to move around and see which of our pals had survived and also to remember the poor lads who had been killed – comradeship is a marvellous feeling and knew no bounds among surviving men.

The company notice board soon made its appearance, and there was no excuse for anybody not reading it. A very important thing happened soon after getting settled in at Launceston. Whereas we had been a part of the 23rd Division in France, we had now been amalgamated into the 50th Northumbrian Division, which was made up of men who hailed from between the two rivers, Tyne and Tees, hence the divisional sign TT. I would become very proud of that shoulder flash as the years went by as the division was to make a name for itself before the end of the war.

The battalion now began to be brought up to material strength with all the paraphernalia of an active service unit to make us quite a formidable force. Weapons we had previously only thought about were now in our possession. The factories were now on a war footing and were doing well. We were given a full complement of Bren guns, Bren carriers, anti-tank weapons, fifteen-hundred weight trucks plus all the backing the division could now provide – we had anything we needed to enable us to take offensive action. So we were now equipped for active service, but we ourselves were far from fit at this time and had yet to undergo some very physical and tactical training.

Up to this time, any kind of serious training had been out of the question and then, out of the blue, came seven days leave, which was more than acceptable to us. It used to be purgatory travelling on the trains in those days; most journeys were undertaken stood in the corridors or perhaps with the luxury of a seat on our kit bag, when there was a constant stream of passing military personnel pushing past to the toilets, and the atmosphere was blue with cigarette smoke. In spite of everything, it was all part of life in the forces and it was a great feeling to be going home, even if only for seven days, but that leave seemed to pass by in a flash.

The first words anybody I knew spoke to me were: 'When are you going back?' During that leave, I don't think I stopped talking because everybody wanted to know about Dunkirk, which was understandable because they must have been very concerned for my safety. But all good things come to an end and it was soon back to the lads. For a short period, as soon as we were back from leave, we started doing route marches, kit inspections and weapon training, amongst other things, to prepare us for life in the army.

Just as we were getting into our stride at Launceston, orders came through for another move; this was early July 1940. Our battalion headquarters was at Hinton Admiral, near Bournemouth, Hampshire. The Companies A, B, C and D were dispersed in different places nearby, but always on the coast. My company, which was B, came off rather well as we were billeted in the grounds of Highcliffe Castle, which was only half a mile from the village of the same name. The officers had the distinct privilege of having rooms within the castle itself and I, being Major Petch's batman, shared rooms with the four other company batmen, in the servants' quarters of the castle. All the other companies were dispersed across different areas near the beaches.

It was a beautiful castle and was still fully furnished to a very high standard; I can see it now, especially the large dining room, with its long, mahogany table, thick carpets, high ceiling and decorated walls. All the other rooms, too, were well furnished, though we were not allowed to use them. I was very sad indeed when, in 1952, I went for a sentimental holiday with my wife and baby girl and discovered the castle to be a very sorry ruin. I returned to the area for many years to reminisce and in 1993 I went for probably my last visit, and lo and behold, building work was going on and I was overjoyed to learn that the castle was being restored.

Back in 1940, the grounds of the castle were extensive and continued by way of sand dunes and a rather steep slope right down to the beach. Most of our time here was taken up preparing beach defences, erecting barbed wire and other obstacles and laying mines on our section of the beach, also by building gun emplacements with sand bags and setting up Bren guns on fixed lines. These positions were manned for twenty-four hours a day and this, of course, was the period of an expected invasion. We felt very confident of our ability to give a good account of ourselves should the enemy try to set foot on our part of the coast. Our earlier confrontations with the Germans had given us the confidence – we had been well blooded in warfare.

Major Leslie Petch, to give him his full name, was a very popular company commander and he was more like a father figure to us all. Really, for a soldier, he was over-generous and sympathetic to our requirements. I recall that one day the bread ration failed to be delivered to the stores and, without hesitation, he sent men into the village to buy all the bread they could get and he paid for it out of his own pocket. Fortunately, he was a rich landowner and well able to afford it; however, his response to the shortage of bread was immediate.

The necessity to keep ourselves fit was paramount, and since route marches were out of the question because of the possible imminence of invasion, we did a good deal of exercise on the beach; we called it PT in those days. We also did running along the beach, when we would be dressed in full marching order with a bag of sand in our pack and would run up and down the sand hills; we were on the verge of becoming fit. Unfortunately, the sea was out of bounds to us or I might have learned to swim.

The ladies of Highcliffe were very tolerant towards us in many ways. Whenever they saw us walking in the village they would ask us to their houses for tea. I particularly remember one occasion when a lady of substantial means asked my pal, Jack Cargill and me if we would like to go to her house for tea. But what a house – it was a very large residence standing in its own parkland. There were several ladies, many of whom were accompanied by their husbands, who were members of the Rotary Club and they gave Jack and me a grand time. We were served tea on a lush lawn sitting on beautiful garden furniture and two maids hovered around us – well, we were young and handsome! They were very genuine hosts and knew how to make a chap welcome.

After tea, we were escorted to another lawn to play croquet, and since this was a very new experience to us young men, we were instructed on the finer points of the game, which we thoroughly enjoyed. We had had an introduction to how the other half lived and it was a nice little interlude from life in the army. Jack was a good pal. I remember during the retreat he opened his mouth too wide to yawn and his jaw locked! After cessation of hostilities, Jack became a Methodist preacher in Stockton, a town near my home.

Some mornings, I had to go into the village to make purchases for Major Petch and a little old lady named Mrs Fish ran one of the shops we patronized. After a while, she asked me to have coffee with her and, only for five minutes, to listen to a short sermon and a hymn on the radio at 0955 hrs every morning. Those five minutes always gave me a great peace of mind.

For the reader who is unaware of the duties of a batman I think I ought to explain them. I did not do guards or fatigues (such as cleaning floors or peeling spuds), but participated in all other soldiery activities, because first and foremost I considered myself to be a good conscientious member of our company. Also, it was paramount that I should keep myself as fit as the other lads – batmen do not win wars. The night duty guards always awakened me at 0530 hrs. I would perform my ablutions, then go to the cookhouse for mugs of tea for the Major and myself. I would go to his room, knock on the door and wait for permission to enter, say, 'Good morning, Sir' and pass a remark about the weather then take my leave. I would then join my pals for breakfast, after which I went back to my room and made up my bed and kit in the regulation manner.

Then it was time to go to the Major's quarters and ask him if he needed anything special doing that day, other than the usual routine. After the company commander had left to attend to his duties, I tidied the room and made up the bed. Unlike the other ranks, the Major always had white bed linen when we were in billets. I polished with vigour whatever shoes had been worn; also the spare Sam Browne belt and, every day, I pressed the spare uniform. That routine usually took me most of the morning, after which I would have a good dinner with the lads before joining my platoon for normal duties.

The Major's wife came to visit him for one week and they stayed in a hotel in the village. She was as much a lady as he was a gentleman, and she thanked me for looking after her husband. Very soon after Mrs Petch had left Highcliffe a most regrettable thing happened. Major Petch was sad to inform us that he was leaving us and in fact was being discharged from the army on medical grounds. We were all stunned as he was so popular with officers and men alike. He had never failed to set a good example of gentlemanly conduct to every one of us. It was said that he had bad eyes, but I was the closest person to him and I knew different. With the benefit of hindsight, Major Petch could never have undertaken a company commander's duties under the conditions which faced us in the future – mentally, most certainly, but physically, I doubt very much, because of his age and weight. He had been a Territorial Army officer and there is a vast difference between that position and doing twenty or thirty-mile route marches under harsh conditions. He often talked to me, things I have forgotten about, but one thing has stuck in my mind from those talks. He was busy signing some documents and he paused and said to me: 'Cheall, always remember, never sign a paper until you have read what you are signing, never take it for granted that what is on that document is what you think is on it.' He shook my hand before he left and said: 'Goodbye, Cheall, and thank you, I will always remember the company.'

As the Major left his beloved men, B Company also vacated its position on the coast. It had been a pleasant interlude and not a bit boring, as life in the army so often was in the future. So goodbye, Highcliffe, Swanage here we come!

Chapter 7

Training Begins

AT THE end of September 1940, we moved to Studland Bay, a quiet seaside village near Swanage, Dorset. Swanage is very hilly; good exercise for our legs as we were constantly on the go. We slept on straw palliasses in the rooms of private hotels, which had been requisitioned for the duration of the hostilities – it was certainly a change from sleeping on the floor.

We started to do a little training – route marches of fifteen and twenty miles in length and small exercises; several times we covered the distance from Swanage to Studland and around Corfe castle and back. Although I now know that the scenery in that area is beautiful, in those days we never thought of it like that, wherever we happened to be billeted. Footslogging was footslogging and that was all there was to it. The only highlight was seeing a German bomber crash near here one day. As at Highcliffe, we were still aware of the danger of invasion; guard duties and beach duties took up much of our time. But these tasks did not mean that the usual army disciplines were relaxed as we were not free agents, but soldiers, and we knew that vigilance could not be relaxed. At any time of day or night a different platoon would receive an invasion alert; talk about scalded cats! We dressed and armed ourselves in record time then fell in on the street and ran like hell down the hill to man the defences on the beach, pier and promenade. There were also gun emplacements on the higher ground overlooking the sea. Some of the lads used to curse a great deal, but still appreciated this was a darn sight better than Dunkirk had been.

The company notice board was very important and woe betide anyone who missed an item which concerned them, such as the list of lads who would be on guard on a particular night – for this we would spend hours cleaning our equipment – polishing boots, and it meant polishing not just cleaning; cleaning the brasses on the webbing; washing – ah – scrubbing the webbing, which is what we called the shoulder straps etc., then blancoing it khaki; pressing trousers; then came the rifle; we always kept this clean but on a guard parade, especially, there were no excuses for a speck of dust.

Strange, but there was always the odd tough guy who didn't give a damn so his turnout wasn't perfect – he hadn't had time to shave or something, then he would be put on a 252. Queer, but usually these were really good lads and in later years, when we were in action, they were the kind of boys who would do something very brave. When one was on guard in England, the day before was free to clean kit, the day after was free to try and rest a little. The guard used to be two hours on and four hours off, for twelve hours. Once again, we were kept occupied with guard duties and beach defences and many things became routine – all part of army life.

General Montgomery had very definite views about the standard of training his soldiers should do their utmost to attain in order to perform the duties that future operations would demand of us. We were to train as we had never done before, and with that objective in mind, at the end of September 1940, we soon moved again – always on the move – to winter quarters at Frome, in Somerset, or rather two miles outside of the town, and here we would be put to the test during the miserable winter of 1940.

All companies of the battalion were billeted here and the Headquarters Company, together with battalion headquarters, had taken over a very large, well-built, old property which must have been owned by a very wealthy landowner. There was a wide, semi-circular drive around the front and rear of the building, and stables and the medical room were at the rear. Other buildings were taken over by the transport section; all the property was standing around a cobbled courtyard. These, then, were our winter quarters, from where we would learn the hard facts of life in the army during wartime. We were destined to do some very intensive training from now on; this had been impressed upon every one of us, including our officers.

It was our first experience of Nissen huts during winter conditions; during the summer they were too hot, but now in the winter they were like refrigerators. When we breathed, our breath made clouds – it was bitterly cold. We had one small round stove in the centre of the stoned floor, which was totally inadequate though the lads who had their beds nearest to it were not so badly off. We used to sleep in our long wool vest, shirt and socks, and with three good army wool blankets. Bed was paradise to us. We used to lie on our bed and sing the song of the day, or somebody would tell jokes. It was always a good laugh, except on one occasion that I can recall. Actually, we had settled down for the night when suddenly the door burst open and a lad who had been drinking fell in, shouting and cursing at everybody, drunk as a lord; he just would not keep himself in order, so three of the tough young lads picked him up, threw him on his bed and said: 'Now keep quiet, yer bugger (only worse) or we'll throw you outside.' That shut him up, but I think he was out for the count. Next morning, he was right as rain and couldn't remember a thing.

Here, for two months, we seemed to be static, as if somebody was wondering what to do with us. Well, they soon let us know! One day, a message was read out to us from General Montgomery in which he stipulated that the V Corps, of which we were a part (we being the 6th Green Howards) must be prepared, by the spring of 1941, to give battle to the enemy wherever they were to be found. We must be able to move many miles in transport, then face a march of twenty or thirty miles and confront the enemy, giving him more than he bargained for; regardless of weather conditions, we would be expected to sort him out.

Training began in earnest and no time was lost in putting orders into action in order to achieve the desired ability to fight as first-class soldiers. We underwent physical training, cross country runs, route marches and pack drill – this was running in full kit. On other days, we would do weapon training, stripping down Bren guns, mortars and anti-tank weapons until we could do it blindfold, naming all parts and function as we handled them.

We had neither illusions about what was expected of us, nor any misapprehension about the intensity of our training at Frome. We had to be determined to reach the peak of fitness and officers and men alike were going to be driven as never before – the playing at soldiers had finished. It was emphasised that we should stretch ourselves and put all our energy into becoming first-class fighting men, and in the process uphold the traditions of the regiment. There was to be no slacking or scrounging and it would be stamped on in no uncertain manner. Nobody was allowed to go sick unless his condition was serious. That little lot gave us plenty to occupy our thoughts. Some of the lads used to play hell and there was no shortage of foul language, but that was all part of the rough life we led; we did not pretend to be angels but they were really grand lads and hard nuts to crack.

To start our day, if we were not going on a route march, reveille was at 0530 hrs, we were awakened by the duty NCO. 'Come on, you lot of pansies, hands off your c---s and outside in fifteen minutes!' Outside, it was a real mean wind, too cold for a brass monkey. The grass was covered in hoar frost, great if that is what you like, but we didn't like. Dressed in shorts and vest, we did a run round the park, or twice if the NCO was in a bad mood, and ended up with exercises, by which time we had a sweat on. Now we could do our ablutions and get our warm long underpants on beneath our battle dress – all our clothes were made of wool.

Breakfast was a ten-minute walk away over the other side of the park, and we were ready for it. Our food was usually very good and wholesome. As an example, for breakfast, we had thick porridge to stick to our ribs, bacon, egg and sausages with plenty of bread and a mess tin full of hot strong tea. In England, I don't ever remember going hungry, which was just as well because we rarely had a canteen or NAAFI. I can't begin to imagine the consequences of a battalion of today's soldiers being billeted in a place where there was no NAAFI or recreational facilities! For tea, we had sardines and a seven-pound tin of jam on the table, always plenty of bread and margarine with tea; we were all good eaters. Strange, I never put weight on. When I was called up at twenty-two years of age, I was ten and a half stone and I was the same weight when I was demobbed six years later and I was very fit.

The weather was mostly atrocious; we never seemed to be dry. Route marches were always done in full marching order, each section of ten men keeping three yards apart, taking turns to carry the Bren gun. We walked for fifty minutes and rested for ten. There was a Second Lieutenant with each platoon consisting of three sections. These marches had to be done, and although there used to be some moaning among the lads, it did not deter us from having a good old singsong while we were stepping it out, and many a time the words were adapted to suit our feelings. It was no use being miserable because we knew the job had to be done and we were rapidly becoming fitter and stronger than we had ever been.

I remember one thirty-mile march we did and we all felt a bit rough during the last five miles when, suddenly, two three-tonners turned up – the regimental band had arrived to accompany us, and we didn't half step it out. I have never forgotten that and, even today, many a time I tap that tune out with my fingers. Arriving back at camp the mobile showers were awaiting us.

Standing out from all route marches and military exercises we did, there was one I will always remember. We were taken by three-tonners to a point on Exmoor – not a very exciting landscape at that time of the year. Bitter cold winds were blowing which cut right through our clothing, good as it was. Then we did a thirty-mile forced march, returning to Exmoor, followed by a mock battle, which lasted through the night, then another fifteen miles march and another exercise which ended up at 1800 hrs, by which time of course it was dark and very wintry. We could not feel our fingers and toes; hell, we were tired. Then up comes the grub and plenty of it – good, substantial, bully stew followed by boiled rice. It was fabulous but we needed it because it was the worst weather that I had ever experienced in the army, and to make matters a great deal worse, it had been snowing for an hour – the prospects were bleak.

Our Sergeant walked amongst us and said, 'Right lads, bed down.' The ground was covered in snow! But we were young, fit and tired and we slept on the ground anywhere. We cleared out our little patches as best we could, put our ground sheet down, and using our faithful small pack for a pillow, covered our weary bodies with two blankets and the waterproof gas cape. Some of the lads slept together so that they had four blankets, and if we hadn't been all in we could not have managed to sleep, conditions as they were.

When we were awakened at 0600 hrs our breath had frozen to the blankets and we all had our own little igloos covering us! We must have been tough in those days, but the sleep had been a tonic and the cooks had sent up a good, hearty breakfast.

During the night, a most dreadful thing had happened a hundred yards away from us. Three lads who had slept too near the roadside, which was barely visible anyway, had been run over by a tank, which had been taking part in the exercise, and nobody had heard anything. The poor kids would not have felt a thing, and only nineteen years of age. We all took it rather badly.

It had been a divisional manoeuvre and all supporting services had been involved. For eighteen hours we had been put to the test in adverse conditions, and everybody concerned had shown the grit and determination not to let the side down; the umpires were all over the place and showed their satisfaction. We had shown our capabilities in mock attack and defence and had not failed.

But the exercise had ended in tragedy; most of us had known those three lads – they had been at Dunkirk with us, and now their young lives had ended. After that incident, the manoeuvres were called off and, believe me, we had to march the thirty miles to the transport, which took us back to camp. We just dumped our kit on our beds and fell in for meal parade and after a good dinner we were beginning to thaw out. Returning to our huts, we sat on our beds and talked, just a little miserable. After a while, somebody said, 'Well, lads, I'm buggered. It's time to get my head down', and we all followed suit.

'Come on lads, out of it!' came the shout. 'Stop dreaming of home or your girlfriends. It's a man's army you're in, not the boy scouts!' There was no running that morning; we all had a shower and tended to our sore feet before, once again, trekking through the frosty grass for breakfast.

'I don't know what is the matter with you all this morning, that exercise was a piece of cake.' That was from one of our officers who was turned out immaculately, and he had been duty officer in camp whilst we had been roughing it on Exmoor. The lads always took that kind of comment in good spirits, as most of our officers knew exactly how we felt and were always understanding about the mood of the men. That is the reason they were so popular and could always depend upon getting that little bit extra out of the lads.

Our training programme had run its course, when we all received a shock. There was a notice on the company notice board to the effect that we had to parade at 0900 hrs next morning. Our Colonel came before us and said that we would all be going on embarkation leave within a matter of days. It came as a bombshell but, of course, it should have been expected – why else had we been training so very hard these past months? Now, we knew. We had reached a peak of fitness as never before.

After we were dismissed, the speculation began. It was usually the married men who felt it the most, but fortunately the majority of us were single boys aged between nineteen and twenty-two, so we just took it in our stride. We all knew at that time where the fighting was taking place, and were certain we would be going to the Middle East.

Next day, at 1100 hrs, there was another compulsory parade. Really, it seemed to be hilarious at the time, but we were fitted out with tropical kit. Within days, everybody was given a thorough examination; then I received a shock. My sinus had been causing me some distress for a while, but now I received confirmation of a problem when the Medical Officer told me that I had chronic sinusitis, and that I would not be going abroad with the battalion. Well, to put it mildly, I was dumbstruck; never having given a thought that I would be leaving the lads under such circumstances; my thoughts and actions had always been most loyal to my company and I was distressed. I had been with most of the lads since April 1939, knew their moods and respected them for what they were – good, honest and sometimes rough Yorkshire lads, who would give their all for each other.

Arrangements were made and I was admitted to Bath hospital for two days, to undergo an operation. I returned to my company for three days and my sinus was very sore, but it was good talking to the lads, and I knew that I was going to miss their crude hilarity, smutty jokes and swearing. They pulled my leg no end, all saying that I was a lucky bugger, but at the time I didn't agree. I was really downhearted. Comradeship in the army is a truly marvellous thing – we were like brothers and would go through hell for each other and the thought of leaving them and going to a lot of strangers was an awful feeling. But as time passed by I knew I had indeed been the lucky one because almost all of them were fated to be killed or captured in North Africa.

While I waited for another posting, I had to move to Richmond, Yorkshire, and I went to the orderly room and collected my travel warrant there. It was only about thirty miles from my home town, but I had heard tales about the Green Howards depot which did not give me a great deal to look forward to. But time would tell. From the back of a fifteen hundred-weight truck I took a very emotional look at the lads and felt the wrench having to leave them as I shouted, 'So long!' as the truck departed for the station. I always remember the names of my pals and officers. Even now, some years later, I can still see them.

As the train travelled north, a kaleidoscope of events which had occurred during the last two years passed through my thoughts, and as a backdrop to these I passed a living picture of the ever-changing English countryside. Richmond is the headquarters of the Green Howards regiment and a chapel there is dedicated to all who have given their lives in war. The residents were very proud of their association with our regiment, which was formed in 1875.

I had never been to Richmond before; I arrived during the third week in May 1941. Here, new recruits were trained from scratch in order to form new battalions. Now then, can I say anything complimentary about our depot? It was in total contrast to beautiful Richmond but, nevertheless, it was where our roots were. It was a large barracks, situated at the top of a hill, Richmond Hill. There was a very large tarmac parade ground, and the whole area looked windswept and inhospitable, which I suppose was to be expected, because regimental depots are not supposed to be places where one can recuperate. As the name implies, depots are where not-so-fit civilians are made to tow the line and are transformed, sometimes against their will, into dedicated soldiers and, just as important, loyal Green Howards, being put through the mill in the process. They usually made pals easily because they were almost all extrovert, which was very important, and they would learn the basics of what life in the infantry was all about from scratch. It was a good job that they did not realize, then, where their lives as soldiers would take them and that life at the depot was really a piece of cake! The infantry was no place for weaklings. It was a hard way of life but the rewards were great – and for better or for worse, that is where my journey from home took me.

I had been in uniform for two years, so the basic training was not for me, it would not make me a better soldier, only a very bored one. My sojourn here would not be very long, just long enough to accumulate a few more memories, and until a posting to another battalion came through. I was more or less, then left to my own devices, which was really no use to me whatsoever, because I was an active individual and needed to be doing things, not lazing about. However, I did the usual drill parades and all the other bull dished out by NCOs and a Regimental Sergeant Major who had never been away from the depot. I did not have any special pals here and was not happy.

Promotion never entered my head up to this time, as I had enjoyed army life doing what we had done, although the going had been tough in the 6th. One day, on the notice board, I read that applications were invited for anybody wanting to become an officer. I applied and had an interview with a committee. Although I was not told in so many words, the one thing that let me down was the fact that I did not have any independent means of income. I was asked that question. This determined me to remain a private for the remainder of the war; though I was asked about promotion I always said, 'No', though I did change my mind twelve months later.

Shortly after this episode, out of the blue, an NCO came up to me and said that the duty officer at the officers' mess wanted to see me. I spruced myself up and went along to see him, whereupon he informed me that he did not think I would be at the depot for long, as I was already an experienced soldier and until such time as a posting came through would I mind helping out in the officers' mess as a waiter since, according to my records, I was associated with officers through my job as batman to Major Petch, so I accepted as it seemed better to keep my mind occupied.

The waiter's job was most interesting while it lasted, but more suitable to a soldier with less qualifications than myself, if I may be so bold as to say as much. I realised that I would soon become soft. I will always remember one Captain who was a little older, as were many of the officers, because the younger commission of men were with the battalions on active service. This officer, when he came into the dining room for breakfast, always came to me to serve him; he would say, 'The usual, Cheall', and he did not mean the usual breakfast; he meant the usual drink – whisky! Every morning was the same; he was a good man but a very silly one too.

The depot was usually administered by soldiers of good character, who had served for some years in the Regular Army and were past the age for active service, which was quite understandable, but they did an excellent job of work in keeping the regimental traditions, and turned out thousands of fit young soldiers. Once a lad had become fitter than he had ever been in civilian life and was surrounded by boys like himself, he realized that the training he had undergone had been a good thing and broadened his outlook on life. Civilian life would seem so far away.

Chapter 8

I Am Posted

I HAD only been at Richmond for a few weeks when my posting came through in about September, for which I was very pleased because I would soon lose my fitness doing a job of work which did not involve any strenuous activity. I had been through the mill in order to attain the standard of fitness I possessed when I was sent to Richmond, and there was no point in letting myself slide backwards health-wise. I was keen to be on the move and to be taking part in the activities of a battalion again as it was a good life for most of the time. This time I travelled a little farther north to join the 11th Battalion, The Green Howards, which was stationed at Gosforth racecourse near Newcastle-upon-Tyne.

The Battalion had been formed very recently, in June 1941, and was made up of recruits from the depot. The commanding officer was Lieutenant Colonel Parry. Almost all the other ranks were young men of nineteen and hailed from all over the North Riding of Yorkshire. It was not destined to be an active service battalion, but to train young soldiers until they reached the required standard of efficiency, before being posted to an active unit – the 4th, 5th, 6th or 7th Green Howards. Men going to these units were always from the North Riding until the latter stages of the war, when the number of young men from the area was drying up.

At Gosforth, the routine was fairly humdrum; just the usual everyday duties; all guards, red tape and drills, not enough to tax the energy of anybody. The training was kids' stuff compared to what I had done in the good old 6th. It all seemed very strange to me for a while, being among so many lads who were younger than me and who had not yet reached a very high standard of efficiency. It took me a little time to settle down, but settle down I did. These were going to be good young soldiers; they had that devil-may-care attitude, which was a good way to be in the army.

I spent much time explaining to them how I came to be amongst them, and the lads I came to know well were curious about what it had been like to be in action at the time of Dunkirk. We had fallen in for a rifle inspection, at the end of which our platoon officer beckoned to me to have a word with him,

'You are new man, Cheall, aren't you?'

'Yes, sir.'

'Well, the company commander wants to see you.'

So off I went, wondering what on earth he wanted me for.

'Cheall, I have been looking at your records, and I see that you were your company commander's batman in the 6th Battalion; not that I am looking for a batman, but it has occurred to me that you might acquit yourself well in a position I have a vacancy for. How does company officers' cook appeal to you?'

It took me about twenty seconds to decide that it did. Right away, he told me that of course he realised there was a difference between a batman and a cook, and so that it would relieve me of any anxiety I might have about cooking, I would be sent on an officers' cooks' course. The one stipulation about being cook was that it would only apply whenever the company was in a different position to other companies; at any other time I would have to be available for normal duties, which suited me very well. The experience would be a challenge to me and I looked forward to the opportunity with the greatest enthusiasm. Also, I would keep in touch with the lads and would not fall behind in whatever my company was doing.

I subsequently went on the cooks' course at Fenham Barracks, which was not far from Gosforth. I soon realized that there was more to cooking than I had imagined, but I came away feeling satisfied that I had learned a great deal and that I had an aptitude for cooking, being confident that my company commander's trust in my ability would be justified. I seemed to have, at the moment, the best of both worlds, as it was good to be in the company among the lads and also I looked forward to cooking, whenever the necessity arose.

After returning to Gosforth, we were there only two more days when we moved further into Northumberland. It was October 1941 and I soon got the chance to show what I had learned about being officers' cook. During this period with the 11th Battalion, we were always billeted in Nissen huts, usually among sandbanks, at Whitley Bay, Seaton Sluice, Seaton Delaval, Cullercoats and Blyth, always on the move. Our duties were to guard the coast, but much time seemed to be wasted, with nothing really constructive being undertaken. It seemed that the powers that be did not know what to do with us, a bit reminiscent of the 6th Battalion during the early days of the war.

We were about to move, yet again. It was January 1942 and for the first time I went to Lincolnshire, but our surroundings had not changed because, once again, we were in Nissen huts amongst the sand at Donna Nook, North Somercoates and Marsh Chapel, still on guard duty, but with a few short route marches thrown in. These lads did not know the meaning of long, forced route marches such as the 6th had done. Things would have to change if these young soldiers were to become fit enough to join one of the active service battalions now overseas.

After several locations, we ended up at a small village called Mareham-le-Fen, still in Lincolnshire, but a few miles from the coast. From Mareham, different platoons were posted for short periods on the coast and every platoon was on duty for two periods guarding Skegness pier, which was very exposed to rough seas and a bitterly cold wind. There is nothing less rewarding than doing a twenty-four hour guard, especially during the night periods, two hours on and four hours off – time seemed endless and of course, in those days, the blackout was strictly enforced. Whilst I was at Skegness, we were billeted in requisitioned private hotels on the sea front, sleeping on the floor. On two occasions I was sent on duty to the Butlins Holiday Camp and found that the place had been taken over by the Royal Navy for training would-be matelots and it was spotlessly clean. Here, we had a concrete pillbox and had to keep a lookout to sea but there was no way that this routine was preparing us for active service. It was getting a bit boring.

Then training then started to take on more significance. At last, somebody seemed to have awakened to the fact that one day, not so far off, these lads would have to go to battalions to replace battle casualties, and that at present something was missing from the training schedules. Route marches of around fifteen miles were undertaken to start with, including such things as walking up to our chests in water and letting our clothes dry on us while we walked. The intensity of weapon training, which was lacking up to now, was speeded up and the firing range came on to the agenda along with map reading and the use of the compass. Most of the lads had only ever fired rifles on a firing range. Now, they were going to learn all there was to know about any weapon which they were likely to come into contact with and to respond instinctively to commands.

Weapon training involved the lads stripping down a Bren machine gun and re-assembling it, and I would time them. In this way we found future Bren gunners. At last, the lads were beginning to realize that there was more to soldiering than guard duties, and more important training started to be done on section and platoon tactical exercises, with more emphasis on deployment under any given circumstance which could possibly arise during battle. One night, we were taken twenty miles away in transport where section leaders were given a compass and compass bearing, then we had to find our way back across country, and through a thick wood, without cheating – it was a challenge accepted in good heart by us all. As a matter of fact, most of this sort of training had not been undertaken by the 6th. I am certain that the lads in the 11th were not as fit as I was when I joined them, but it would come.

In the middle of all this activity, my platoon commander proposed to put my name forward for a stripe, which I took, and I was then section leader (Lance Corporal). I had never sought promotion because I did not want to drift away from the friendship of the lads; this was always very important to me, but they all knew me well enough now to know that I would do my best for the section. My responsibilities increased accordingly; I enjoyed the routine and I had good lads in my section, which was number two. I took my promotion seriously and I still have my notebook containing the names of the lads in my section and platoon.

Mareham was only a village and we didn't have a NAAFI or even a canteen, so during off-duty hours the opportunity for outside activity was non-existent apart, that is, from going to the local pub, where our constant problem was money. Many of our evenings were passed by talking or playing cards on our beds (we didn't have a table or chairs) writing letters, or having a singsong. Bear in mind that we didn't even have a radio in those days. I remember one incident vividly. One evening, some of us were writing letters and a boy wrote to his mother; two days afterwards he received a letter – he had only put his own name and address on the envelope and we didn't half pull his leg! Oh yes, there was plenty of opportunity to have a bit of fun. Believe it or not, I passed a lot of time away, during spare hours, darning socks for the lads and I used to shorten trousers for my mates; our clothes were never the right size when they were issued. I think that being a little older than most of the lads caused them to look up to me and I appreciated that.

During the whole of the time I was in the army, I can only ever remember being in one camp when we had a NAAFI, so it was hard luck if we wanted any supper. I was on good terms with the cooks here, because they knew that I had been on the cooks' course at Fenham and could talk shop, with the result that I was able to scrounge bread and a tin of jam for supper for the lads in my hut.

Also, from Mareham, we could go to the cinema – three miles' walk each way. Three or four of us would go and step it out, singing our heads off while we were walking – it was good. I think that here we all worked hard, ate well, played a little and got a good night's sleep. We were billeted in this area for some time.

Sometimes, when I was lying stretched out on my bed with my hands under my head, I would think about life in the army, of the past two or three years and wonder about the lads in the 6th battalion, where they were and what they were doing. After all, they were my first mates and even now in 1994 I remember their names.

As the middle of November drew near, I was looking forward to going home for Christmas, but an event occurred which precipitated any thought of that coming about.

Chapter 9

To the Middle East

THE PASSAGE of time in the army became so repetitive and monotonous that at times everybody became browned off, but these were only passing phases which comradeship quickly dispelled. It was the third week in November 1942 and rumours were circulating that some of us were going to be put on a draft for overseas, though of course, no information had been given to us for reasons of security. The rumour did not exist for long because a list soon went up on the company notice board, giving the names of those lads who would be on it. My name was one of about fifty who could expect to be going; we all looked to see if our pals were on it; it did not seem so bad if we were all together, and my two particular pals were included.

Anybody who has not experienced comradeship as it existed in the forces during the war really has missed something in life. Although we could not be told, we all sensed that we would be going to the Middle East to join one of The Green Howard battalions, but a shock awaited us in that respect. Within days, we were going on nine days' embarkation leave.

For relatives, this kind of leave was most welcome – which was quite natural – wondering if they were seeing their loved one for the last time, and this was a distinct possibility. Soldiers, as a rule, were not too concerned about overseas duty; we were young and enthusiastic and going abroad held no fears for us at that time; it was all part of the job and accepted with good spirit but there was no way that we could persuade our families to have the same enthusiasm as we had about us being sent overseas. That was one of the hazards which everybody who had sons or husbands in the forces had to contend with; consequently there were many broken hearts when the time came for us to return to our units.

At Mareham, there had been a great deal of frenzied activity and in no time at all we had fallen in on the road which ran alongside the camp and were being given a pep talk by the CO. Next morning, it was drizzling with rain and at 0730 hrs on 19 December we were on our way, marching along with our kit bags on our shoulders to the railway station, and the start of an unforgettable experience from which many good lads would not return, but on that day who knew what the future held for us.

I have to say here that I lost my Lance Corporal's stripe as it would not be acceptable for a Lance Corporal to go into action overseas and be expected to take command of a section of men who had already seen action in the desert many times; he would be out of his depth, regardless of his confidence. Still, I didn't mind one bit – I knew what happened to NCOs in action, they were knocked off quick by snipers!

There was a great deal to be learned about fighting in the desert and lads fresh out from England would have to learn pretty fast when the time for action came. I therefore understood why I had been reverted to private and looked forward with anticipation to seeing the lads in my old battalion, once again, in the Middle East. As all soldiers will know, during train journeys, some played cards, some slept, but almost always a mouth organ would be produced and we would have a good old singsong. We had some really good, carefree times in the army, as well as the very sad occasions we had to face in the future. That is how it had to be and that is what gave us the individual characters to do the duty which a soldier was called upon to do.

We had no idea where our troop train was heading for, but as we travelled farther north through Lincoln, Harrogate, Newcastle and Edinburgh we felt that we could not be far from our destination. At each stop we would all pile out on to the platforms to fill our mess tins with tea and to stretch our legs and also to notice that the Red Caps (military police) were on the alert. I am not sure why, but none of the lads could say anything good about them. Most of us wouldn't dream of committing a wilful offence, but of course I suppose there could be the odd lads who didn't want to go overseas and could go absent.

We were on Waverley Station, Edinburgh, for about one-and-a-half hours, where we had a hot meal. I will never understand why we didn't get tired of bully stew.

On our way again, and we arrived at Glasgow at about 0600 hrs next morning, on 20 December. I had never been this far north before, or even to Scotland, so it was all new to me. People in those days just did not travel as they do today. From Glasgow, we travelled to Gourock, on the Firth of Clyde and the docks were crowded with ships of all sizes. It was a bitter cold morning and there was a slight mist. We were no sooner off the train than lighters (small boats, a bit like coal barges) were ferrying us towards the centre of the harbour to a very large ship, which dwarfed everything around it. To see the words *Queen Mary* on the bows of the ship was almost beyond my comprehension. It seemed almost impossible that we were to go overseas on such a majestic ship. I had never imagined that I would ever see the *Queen Mary*, let alone travel on it, and I felt very proud to be British.

We boarded the ship through wide doors at the side of this cavern of a ship and the size of the interior fascinated me. Remember, I had never been on a ship so large. I was to discover that there were eleven decks, and that fifteen thousand personnel were packed into it. Each party had its own quarters, and notices had been posted in the passageways, giving directions to those areas – on those long corridors and staircases one could easily get lost on the ship. The floors had been covered with special flooring to give protection against our army boots, although when we had settled in we changed to denims and sandshoes. We each had a hammock and were rather crowded, but there was plenty of room on other parts of the ship. My two pals and I managed to get places near each other; they were John Bousfield and Arthur Oxley – they were only nineteen and came from Stockton-on-Tees, which was only six miles away from my own home town of Middlesbrough, so we had much in common to talk about, but more of those two lads later. Looking back to those days, we still did not know for where we were bound; this was the one time we could have been told because there was no danger of us telling anybody ashore – we just lived each day as it came.

We sailed on 23 December 1942 and without an escort, which surprised us, but we were told that the ship's speed made it unnecessary. All I could feel and hear was the steady powerful throb of the engines and the rise and fall of the ship as we headed out into the Atlantic. It was not very long before we were feeling most miserable – anybody who has never been seasick cannot have a clue how rotten it makes one feel. Well, despite the size of the ship, the speed of it was causing it to toss about quite a bit, consequently we were all very seasick and it was awful. I was sick for three days and didn't care whether I lived or died; that's how bad it was. Christmas had been and gone before I recovered. I will never forget Christmas 1942. My best pal, John, and another pal, Norman Young, had it really bad. I looked after them both, feeding them and putting them to bed, as the sickness can play havoc with your strength.

We gradually became used to the roll of the ship as it cut through the water, and began to explore the ship and only then realized how large it was. The boat deck and the engine room were out of bounds. The cabins had been largely removed and the hammocks hung three-high between uprights and the passages between the hammocks were three feet wide – I dread to think what would have happened had we been torpedoed. There were two very large dining rooms, one of which was a boarded-over swimming pool. There were three sittings in each of the dining rooms; we were all given a card to show when collecting our meal from the cafeteria and the food was excellent and plentiful.

The only training we did was strenuous exercise on the open deck, which would be eighteen feet wide along the length of each side of the ship and it had windows all along the seaward side. There was no way we could do any other kind of training as we were too crowded, but we put white shorts on and walked for hours. We also sat around a great deal, particularly on the promenade deck, which was long and wide with large windows running the whole length. We would laze around – talking, playing cards or singing; some would have a wrestle for fun. We also played housey-housey (bingo). I remember that John, Norman and I used to go to the housey, run by the canteen, when we had any money; it used to take one penny, though we were almost always broke. Housey took place on the large landing which was atop a wide staircase in front of the canteen and that landing became my haunt as I sat there (on the floor – no chairs) for many hours reading and writing or just thinking. I made myself a pair of white shorts out of a piece of material I found. My pals always knew where to find me – on top of that landing.

There was a first-class canteen and everything on sale, including chocolate and sweets, was produced in the USA. The only trouble was that we never had enough cash.

I would never forget this trip, but at the same time I knew we must have been heading for Egypt and to the realities of war – that fact was inescapable, though even the thoughts of what the future might hold never gave me any reason for concern.

One morning, after we had returned to our quarters from breakfast, our Sergeant told us that we had to gather on the promenade deck in our usual place at 1000 hrs, because Captain Cullan had something to say to us. After we had saluted him, he told us to sit down in a half circle, when he proceeded to say: 'Now then, lads, what I have to say will affect some of you more than others, but the plain fact is that you are no longer Green Howards. I say that with regret, because I know that many of you are loyal to your regiment and have a great regard for your fellow county men. The East Yorkshires are in need of replacements, for reasons you will well know, so it has been decided that this draft will transfer to that regiment as from 30 December 1942. I have been told to explain the need and have done so. Sorry, men.'

It was well-understood by officers that almost all Green Howards at this period in the war came from the North Riding, but I believe that the people at the War Office had the impression that we had something to do with Robin Hood. I was deeply disappointed as I had been looking forward to meeting up once again with the lads of the 6th Battalion. I had always been a Green Howard and proud of it, a good North Riding regiment – we were all Yorkshire lads from around the same area and this was very important to us. But we had to accept it and cursed about it and were not happy. Once again, we were just numbers to be shuffled around.

We were actually told with great understanding, by the officer, the unavoidable reasons for the decision that when men came out of England, they were put into regiments which needed reinforcements – it happened to be the East Yorks. I was annoyed about that, but funnily enough never did get issued with a badge.

I was always an early riser and would walk for miles around the ship, exploring other decks whilst my mates were all still asleep and really enjoyed it. There was one thing I loved to get up early for – I am sure I saw the sun rise every morning; it was magnificent – the sunset likewise, I've never seen anything like it. On one of my walks I became acquainted with a member of the crew and I told him that I must have been all over the ship apart from the engine room, whereupon he said that he would have a word with his superior about me. So, next morning, I made it my business to walk where I knew I would see this man; he too was looking for me. Consequently, he took me to see the engine room. It was like a dream; everything was so spotlessly clean. The engines would not have been out of place in a cookhouse and the engineers were all most sociable, having been told of my curiosity. It was incredible that what I was looking at was driving the huge ship and its human cargo. I could not take in the enormity of it. This was an experience I knew I would never forget, the deep throb reverberating through the ship – but nothing would make up for the sad events waiting to happen.

Boat drill was twice weekly and something not to be missed, because it was within the bounds of possibility that our lives could depend upon it. We would be walking around the ship when, all of a sudden, the alarm would sound at any time of day, then we would make our way, without running, to the appropriate place. All passages and staircases were wide and there were watertight doors everywhere. Remember, there were fifteen thousand landings, so we had to careful not to wander, during the day, too far from our own areas. Fortunately, we had a safe passage down the Atlantic and even though there seemed to be plenty of lifeboats and Carley floats covering boat deck, a disaster in the making could have been waiting for us if a U-Boat had been around. It made me think about my brother Jack, who was in the Royal Navy aboard HMS *Gorelston*.

We arrived at Freetown on 29 December and anchor was dropped about half a mile from the harbour coastline. It was a lovely sunny morning and almost as soon as we stopped the natives came all around us in their canoes, singing their songs and offering us bananas and other fruit – I don't know why, as it was impossible for us to reach them as we were six decks up from the water line! This was our first sight of the continent of Africa; it was almost impossible to believe that such a short time ago we were billeted in a small village in Lincolnshire. Nobody was allowed ashore except the officers, who had business to conduct concerning the voyage.

Next morning, I felt the ship begin to move. I went aloft and looked at Africa fade away into the distance.

New Year's morning, 1943, saw me was sitting on the landing at 0700 hrs with no money in my pocket as usual. I used to sit and make notes a great deal when I was sitting alone on that landing. I remember that one patrol I was on in France was very dangerous and we could have easily been taken prisoner, so I destroyed all the notes I had in my pocket as it was against the rules to keep a diary. I wrote many of these notes at the time of the event happening and have just rewritten them, though I kept some of the originals.

The passage from Freetown was an unforgettable journey, which I would love to make again. Every morning, as soon as it was light, around 0630 hrs, I would go aloft and make my way to the stern of the ship and gaze way down at the sea, the screws turning the water like huge egg whisks leaving a wide wake behind us – the endless sea, nothing in sight except for some flying fish on the starboard. But the most impressive sight was the sunrise when, upon a calm sea, that great red ball – the sun – seemed to be rising out of the water. The beautiful sunsets too had a fascination for me; they were creations of the Almighty.

On this leg of our journey, the sea was very rough and it was incredible how much such a huge vessel could be tossed about. Thank goodness we had our sea legs, but the mood of the sea was ever changing and for most of the journey it was tranquil. We arrived at Capetown on 5 January 1943. Looking at the panorama of Capetown was awe inspiring, to be part of my catalogue of memories. It was a beautiful morning and we were allowed on boat deck and stern in order to obtain a grandstand view of the city.

Running up from behind the harbour in the foreground and middle distance – on rising ground – were rows of large white stone buildings, all built on the hillside, which became steeper until it became a mountain – Table Mountain – long and flat as the name implies. It was an inspiring sight and had mountain peaks on each side of it. That night, I watched the sunset from Capetown. It was a great sadness that many of the boys admiring Capetown would not be alive to remember it – what a dreadful thing war is. That other great liner, *Queen Elizabeth*, was also at anchor a little distance away from us, and just to gaze across the water at that magnificent vessel was just like a dream.

Stores were brought aboard and at 0400 hrs on the morning of 7 January 1943, the engines commenced their gentle throb and we sailed away from Capetown, the whole ship trembling slightly and it was a comfortable feeling.

The *Queen Mary* had now been our home for two weeks and we were becoming soft but that would change – this was merely an interlude. The water was still cool and the sea rough as we went around the Cape of Good Hope. In those far off days, none of us knew how long the journey would be to Egypt – which is where we felt our destination was.

Our next sighting of land soon came on the starboard side – it was Madagascar, though we only saw the coastline. It was interesting because I remembered learning about the country at school and it had always had a fascination for me. The sun was very hot as we headed for the Horn of Africa and we were soon dropping anchor at Aden, but our stay here was only 24 hours. Being a large British Naval base, it was a hive of activity. Aden seemed to be a very ordinary place, leaving nothing much to remember it by. Whenever the ship stopped, I always went aloft with absorbing enthusiasm. An end had to come to this idleness and I knew, or rather thought I knew, that an uncertain future lay before us – in about three months many of the lads would be dead.

After leaving Aden, the 1450 miles of the Red Sea lay before us and thence to our destination, where we would join the Eighth Army. So we were on our way again and we continued north, sometimes in sight of the coastline of Italian Somaliland and Eritrea. It was on the Monday morning that we arrived at Suez, where we stayed only briefly. After our journey up the Red Sea we were nearing the end of a three-week journey; then we arrived at Port Tewfik which is situated at the southern end of the Suez Canal and was a hive of industry, with many Royal Navy ships and merchant ships, large and small, anchored in the large bay, bringing supplies for the Eighth Army. The *Queen Mary* had hardly stopped when the ship's tannoy came to life, preparing us for disembarkation, and very soon we were walking over the threshold of the doors in the side of the ship, from magnificence to poverty and onto lighters to take us to the dockside.

These past three weeks had been a revelation to me and I had absorbed as much about the journey as I could, otherwise I could not be writing about it now, fifty-two years later. I took a long lingering look at the majestic *Queen*. How impressive she looked out there in the bay; I would never see her again. Even now, after so many years, I get very nostalgic whenever, on very few occasions, I hear the ship mentioned. She was and still is a beauty. I imagine myself walking along the prom deck or standing at the stern watching the sunrise or sunset. It was an incredible experience.

Chapter 10

Egypt, The Desert

WE STOOD with all our kit, chatting on the dockside, waiting for transport. It materialised in the form of Arab buses which had seen better days, and we were soon on our way to God knows where. I could not possibly have imagined that Egypt was like this. We seemed to have stepped back in time – I don't know how many years. My first impressions of this backward country were most unfavourable. The Arabs appeared to be surviving just as their forebears had done, living in squalid filthy huts on the sand. Dozens of thin, scruffy children were everywhere and scrawny animals were roaming around freely. I wondered where the hell the army had brought us. Fortunately, we got to know better parts of the country later on.

Before we could bat our eyes, we were on army trucks heading for, we knew not where – that was always a most frustrating thing with the army, nobody ever told us where we were bound – we just arrived. No one said, 'Now look, lads, we are doing so-and-so', until D-Day, then it changed. We went via Suez and Ismailia then alongside the Sweetwater canal. We ended up at a large, tented camp about a mile west of the Suez Canal, which was the main British military base in Egypt, Qassasin Camp, and it was indeed just that, there were very few brick-built buildings. Qassasin was described as 'that bugbear of all British troops newly arrived in the Middle East.' It was alleged, if you hadn't already got 'jippy tummy', this was the place you could expect it.

The weather now was very hot. Very quickly, we dumped our kit in a tent allocated to us and went to another tent where we were issued with khaki drill shirts and shorts to wear in a place of our denims. If you could have seen those shorts, well, they were good for a laugh but they were cool in the scorching sun; they had a double buckle fastening at the waist and wide legs which reached almost to our knees, they must have been kept in stock since the Indian campaigns!

We now made our way to another large tent, which was the dining hall. Trestle tables and forms were set out, which was certainly an improvement. Our first meal in Egypt was a disaster. I could not hazard a guess as to what kind of meat it was, but even worse were the mashed green, sweet potatoes. I went hungry that day and many days. I became anxious about my weight, because I was only a slight ten-and-a-half stones and I was now twenty-four years of age. Fortunately, the food did improve.

I think even the flies were pleased about that; there were swarms of thousands of them and even when we were eating or drinking they would settle on our lips and we had to constantly wave them off our food. I don't know how we avoided disease and I reckon I must have had an iron constitution – give me good army grub, cooked by good army cooks, any day!

The huge, tented camp was in the desert, the inhospitable desert – no give, just take. Our billets, again, were square tents just about large enough to hold twenty of us. They had three-foot walls, which had to be rolled up every day so that sand blew right through and covered everything; the whole military base was set on sand. There was a brick-built cinema and another large tent, which was the canteen. I remember one particular thing about the canteen. When I first went in a soldier was playing a piano and he played a tune I had not heard before – Warsaw Concerto. It made me think of home and I have never forgotten that time.

There were no other amenities, whatsoever, and we were some miles from the nearest town of Ismailia. Still, we made our own fun and a great deal of our spare time was passed talking, telling jokes and having a laugh and much time was passed writing letters and, at a later date, airgraphs – one page letters, which, after being photographed and censored, were reduced in size to about 5 x 4 inches to reduce bulk for transit purposes.

Very soon we started a training programme, and in order to get us used to the desert heat and sand, we did much route marching into the desert up and down the dunes, mile after mile. First, it was ten miles, then fifteen and twenty and we could only use our water bottles when our officer said so – that was all part of our initiation to desert conditions and to any circumstances we might have to face in the future. The sun beat down mercilessly during those marches and yet, at night it was always cold. But with day-after-day of scorching hot sun, we soon became used to it and our bodies quickly tanned.

At weekends, anyone off-duty could get army transport to Ismailia. My pals and I made a few trips there; it was a fairly large place but not very clean. There was no entertainment but it was a change of surroundings. I remember young boys who haunted off-duty soldiers to buy obscene post cards.

The strangest thing happened during one trip into the town. When I was billeted at Mareham-le-Fen, one lad in my section was called Ernie Booth who lived at Glossop, in Derbyshire. Well, as I was walking in Ismailia, whom should I bump into but Ernie. That lad had come out to the Middle East on a later draft than me and had been posted to the Durham Light Infantry and yet here we were meeting again in Ismailia! I then lost touch. Forty years later, I received a telephone call and the caller wanted to know if I was ever stationed at Mareham in 1942. Again, Ernie Booth had come into my life and of course we remained in touch. He had been wounded during his first action at Primosole Bridge in Sicily and ended his war in Egypt.

The powers-that-be were calling for volunteers for the paratroops, and a display was being held to encourage the would-be paratroopers to transfer from their present regiment. My pal and I went along and were impressed enough to think about it. I am pleased that 'think' is all we did, as I am sure that I would have ended up in the deadly fiasco at Arnhem, which never should have been. I obviously took part in many actions and skirmishes, but Arnhem was dreadful. So instead, I took a course to learn to manoeuvre a Bren carrier. This was a lightly armoured, tracked vehicle used for carrying half a dozen men and it had a Bren gun fixed to the front end. It was a good course and gave me an insight into the capabilities of that workhorse. Well, I passed the test, learning to control the carrier up the steep sand dunes to almost a point, and then topple forward down the other side. On roads, the vehicle could travel at 40mph and to drive a Bren carrier fast across the desert and up and down large sand hills, at speed, was an exhilarating experience. Mind you, if there were any German 88mm guns around it would be a different matter altogether.

For a while, we had to guard thousands of German prisoners of war, who had been taken at Alamein. They looked really exhausted and were almost all about the same age as us and wanted to be sociable; it was not their fault they were at war and they seemed very pleased to have been taken prisoner. We would take out small working parties about the camp doing maintenance. Two of the young Germans in my party spoke very good English and were quite well educated, wanting to make conversation and I, rightly or wrongly, obliged. Their names were Helmut Beckermeyer and Alfred Decker, both from Bremen in northern Germany. They told me all about their families and homes and gave me their addresses. I formed the opinion that not all Germans were bad, the same as not all English are good, because I had come across some awful characters in my time in the army. Granted, we were at war, but I felt that if I had been a prisoner of war I would have appreciated my guard showing me some kindness, so my favourable reaction to the young Germans was to give them little treats, like biscuits and chocolate. These were soldiers just like us – Wehrmacht not SS. Eventually, I wrote a letter to the parents of those boys, telling them that I had met their sons and that they were alive and well and happy to have been taken prisoner. Apparently, they had not known this news. The mother of Alfred Decker wrote back thanking me for my kindness and sent me their only photograph of Alfred. I still have the letter and snap among my souvenirs. God had been good to me and I felt I was upholding my faith by being kind to those lads, and I never regretted the action I took.

The letter read as follows:

Dear Mr Cheall

I am glad I am finally able to thank you for what you have done for me. It was very kind of you to forward your son's letter to me and thanks to you I learned he was alive and felt well. But unfortunately he did not know himself anything about our fate … I am so happy he found in you a man who could understand him so well.

Now he is asking me to send him a photo of his. You can imagine it is not easy to part with the only picture of my son that I have got, but since Alfred wrote me you have treated him as a comrade, I will fulfill his wish. I am hopeful that my son will soon be released and we shall see him again. Should you ever be in Bremen, you will always be welcome in my home.

Yours sincerely

Sender: Family W Borsinsky (Alfred Decker's Mother)

Bremen

By late March 1943 I was almost black with the heat of the sun. We had been in Egypt for two months and were wondering why we had been sent out here to the Middle East, only to be messing about. It seemed that this was all we were doing, but ours was not to reason why, though the routine we had gone through those past weeks had been an experience I would always remember. We had all now become used to the conditions at Qassasin; even the food had shown some improvement, but the flies persisted in being a torment and thrived on the sweat of our bodies. We had not been forgotten, though; things were soon to get moving. All of a sudden, orders were issued, preparing us for a move.

There was a war being fought and the time had come for us to take part in the action. Very few of the lads at Qassasin had been in any sort of action against the enemy, so they really had no idea what they were going to have to face in the very near future. At least, having been at Dunkirk, I had a good idea what to expect, although this time I expected the Germans to be on the receiving end.

Chapter 11

Back to the Green Howards

WE HAD now been toughened up and had got used to the heat, and at last, orders came through for a move. Our platoon Sergeant came into the tent with orders for us to get it organised in readiness for a move the next day and there were no questions about our destination.

Most of these young lads were full of confidence and high spirits and had not yet been initiated into the realities of facing a ruthless enemy. I had been with the BEF in France and had not forgotten all the whys and wherefores and knew when to keep my head down and when to be aggressive. But when the time came, they had the opportunity to show what stuff they were made of and quickly adapted to the situation in which they had found themselves and, back in those days, none of them showed any reluctance, whatsoever, about going forward to join front line units. Anyhow, it was not before time that we took our leave of this fly-ridden place. We climbed onto the three-tonners and were soon on our way to Cairo airport.

Travelling through Cairo was an experience never-to-be-forgotten. It was a bit of a nightmare for the drivers; simply masses of people and vehicles and there did not appear to be many rules of the road. I had never before seen so many people in one place. Of course, it was the first time that I had had the dubious pleasure of being in a Middle Eastern city, but it was soon left behind us as we headed for the airport.

At the airport, we were each weighed with our kit. There would be about one hundred of us on the draft; groups of twenty were assigned to Dakota aircraft, ten on each side of the plane and we sat on a wooden bench. It was all new to me, in fact, I think, to all of us; we just had not flown before, but in the army so many new experiences were encountered that we just took them in our stride. I do recall the flight was very bumpy. Soon after we had taken to the air we passed over the Pyramids and Sphinx, which I had previously read about. However, we were not on a sight seeing trip, but flying to join the Eighth Army. The flight was uneventful as our RAF had, at this time, mastery of the air.

Landing at Benghazi to refuel, stretch our legs and have some sardine sandwiches and tea, we had a little time to look around and see the devastation of war, which had gone back and forth over this ground during the past two years. Burnt-out vehicles and tanks were everywhere together with piles of rubble, which had once been buildings.

Back onto the plane and onto our destination, Tripoli, capital city of Libya. The landing almost ended in disaster, because shell holes pockmarked the runway, the fighting having passed this way only recently. As our plane touched down, the pilot, good as he was, could not avoid one of the craters. Fortunately, we had lost speed, but even so the plane tipped over to an angle of forty-five degrees, bending the propeller and throwing us all forward, but it was our kit bags that saved any of us from injury. Some of the lads had been asleep and had received a rude awakening and, soldiers being what they are, the air was blue with bad language.

It was not far off dusk when we crawled out of the plane and sorted our kit, then walked across the tarmac to an aerodrome. No time was lost in bringing on the rations; so different from Dunkirk and so well organised. We had a meal and sat talking about the flight and also what our next move might be. Somebody then started to play a mouth organ, which never failed to set us all singing, and the songs of the day usually made us all think of home, the married men about their families, and we would all think about tomorrow. It had been a long day and we soon settled down for the night; sleep came easy.

We had excellent NCOs in those days and we all got on well with them. Next morning, the Sergeant awoke us all to say that we would be here for two days to await orders as to our next move. As soon as we had eaten, a new order was given to pack up and get cracking across the fields to a tented camp, which was about two miles from Tripoli; our time would be ours to do as we wished.

We were allowed into the city, which did not appear to have suffered much by the passage of war; this was where Rommel had come ashore to chase the British out of Africa, which of course he almost did. However, the dockside and harbour installations had been almost completely destroyed by the retreating enemy. German and Italian ships lay wrecked and part sunken in the water at all kinds of angles. The RAF had created hell for the Germans who were now paying the penalty for their wrong doings. The harbour would take some clearing before it could be used to shorten our supply lines.

Now back at camp, we enbussed once more to another destination, but moving ever nearer to the front line, travelling over the very ground upon which fierce battles had so recently taken place. It was 28 March 1943 as we passed through Medenine and then Mareth where, unknown to us at the time, 69th Brigade with 50th Division, my former Division, had fought so magnificently against fierce enemy resistance. My old 6th Battalion had played a very significant part in the fighting for Mareth and had suffered many casualties, together with the other units of the 69th Brigade.

Passing through Gabes, where the name signs were still in place, it seemed hardly possible that Qassasin was almost two thousand miles away. We were now in southern Tunisia where we came to a halt and debussed to await further orders. We then marched about ten miles across country and came to a rest in a clearing among the sand dunes waiting for orders. Almost within the hour we were being sorted; there must have been about five hundred of us going as reinforcements to 50th Division, but at this time I was in the East Yorks.

A Jeep arrived and an officer came towards us and I recognised him at once; he was Captain Carmichael and the last time I had seen him was at Frome in Somerset, with the 6th Green Howards when he was the Transport Officer. Since in the past I had been company commander's batman, I knew all the officers and they knew me. Now we had to fall in – in threes. The Captain walked along the line and a Corporal was with him. Coming closer, the officer looked us all over, thinking his own thoughts, probably along the lines, 'Poor lads, more cannon fodder', because he would realise that most of the new draft had never seen any action. The Captain had come to collect soldiers to replace casualties in the 5th East Yorkshire Regiment and the 6th and 7th Green Howards. Captain Carmichael was a very popular officer among the lads and never flaunted his position. When he came to me he recognised me at once and said: 'Well, well, Cheall, you have caught up with us at last.' I replied that I was afraid I hadn't and that I had been in the East Yorks since December and was not very happy about it. I knew the man and I could talk to him like that. 'That is no problem, Cheall, I can do something about that'. Then he said to the Corporal, 'Transfer this soldier to the 6th Green Howards, with immediate effect.' It was just as easy as that, and my army record card shows that it happened on 29 March 1943. I was lost for words and just said 'Thank you, Sir. It is good to be back in the Green Howards', and he passed on. I could hardly believe it. It meant leaving the pals I had made in the 11th Battalion and on the *Queen Mary*, but in the army one became used to that.

Strange as it may seem, I never saw the Captain again, although I remained with the Green Howards for another eighteen months. I wonder if he survived the war. I went into C Company and, regretfully, I was separated from my pals. John Bousfield and Norman Young went to the 5th East Yorks and Arthur Oxley to the 6th Green Howards, but not in my platoon. John and Arthur were fated to be killed very soon, but more of that later.

So, the esprit de corps of the British Army had cropped up again and it was a great feeling to be a Green Howard once again. Those of us who had been transferred to the 6th battalion departed and marched about three miles to the area where the 6th were taking a rest, which they certainly deserved. They were just lazing about and looking very miserable and tired. At the time we had no means of knowing that they had just taken part in the fierce battle of Mareth where bitter confrontations with the enemy had caused devastation to their numbers. Only the lads who have been involved in an action where they have seen their comrades blown to smithereens know what it is like; nobody else can even begin to imagine what a boy goes through. Some lads just take it all in their stride; others, for a time, dwell upon their experience.

Looking over the faces of the tired lads, they showed signs of strain, which was quite understandable. Although I had been in the 6th for two years and had known many of the lads by name and more by sight, I could hardly believe that I did not recognise anybody. But it was C Company I was now in and I had previously always been in B, but the fact that I did not know anybody held no significance at the time.

After I had been designated a platoon and section and time was free for a while, I decided to wander over to B Company to find some of my old mates who I had known since Territorial Army camp in 1939; I was stunned by what I found. They were all strangers to me, except one. Harry Simpson had been a company commander's batman in England and remembered me, of course.

He seemed very depressed and gave me the impression that he needed a rest from the trauma of battle. When I asked him how come I did not recognise anybody, he said: 'Well, Bill it is good to see somebody I know from the old days and since it might do me good to unburden myself, I will tell you what has happened to the 6th that you remember.' I found it to be a very sad and unbelievable story.

The 69th Brigade of 50th Division left England from Gourock on 3 June aboard HMT *Mooltan*, in a convoy escorted by cruisers and destroyers and at one time an aircraft carrier. They called at Freetown, as did all convoys, remaining from 16 to 20 June, but nobody was allowed ashore. The company then continued to Durban (South Africa) arriving on 4 July. All troops disembarked for seven days. Apparently, this was a happy time as the South Africans were generous and very friendly.

The voyage then continued on board HMT *Mauritania*, arriving at Port Tewfik on 21 July 1942, where they stayed at Qassasin camp. They remained there until 7 August, when they set sail for Famagusta, Cyprus, embarking upon destroyers. In Cyprus they began intensive training in the mountain and preparing defence works at Limassol (Greece and Crete having recently fallen to the enemy). They prepared defence works, then continued training in the form of long tactical marches over mountain tracks and choking white dust. All training was geared to make the lads prepared in case the Germans invaded the island.

In November the battalion moved to Palestine. On 28 November, because of the war situation, the division was on the move again, to Persia. More defence preparation and more training until the end of January 1943, but only for two weeks. On 12 February, the 69th Brigade arrived at a camp near Alexandria. The next day it moved again to Acroma near Tobruk (getting nearer the action). On 22 February, the 6th went into the line of battle. For some weeks, they prepared defences and sent out recce columns into the desert, sometimes for three days at a time. There were casualties and some were taken prisoner. They were constantly on the move in the desert and conditions were dreadful. On 30 May, the battalion moved yet again – new positions and defence works to prepare under fire from the enemy and the elements in the form of hot dust storms.

The water ration was two pints a day for all purposes (try it sometime). Here, they were attacked by the enemy and suffered many casualties, but our lads counter-attacked and were successful. They were constantly on the move in the desert, taking part in many battles, and eventually most of the brigade, (5th East Yorks, 6th and 7th Green Howards) took up defensive positions in what were called boxes, so that all sides could be defended.

Owing to the way that the war was going at the time, the enemy were far better equipped than we were; better anti-tank guns and larger tanks carrying formidable 88mm and the dreaded mobile 88mm, which served as anti-tank, anti-aircraft or artillery piece, using different kinds of shell. Having a superior quantity of weapons, the Germans surrounded the box and to cut a long story short, before the British surrendered, many had been killed. The remainder (apart from some who managed to escape) were taken prisoner at Gazala. That is the story I was told by Harry so no wonder I did not see any faces I recognised.

At that time, the Germans played havoc with our desert army. That is roughly what happened to the 6th, but it was re-formed. Had I stayed with them, the chances of my being here today would have been remote! Almost all of the rebuilt battalion consisted of replacements for those who had been killed or captured in the Gazala battle in the desert, in the days when things were going against us. That would have been my fate if I had not left my unit in 1942 because of my sinus trouble.

After talking to that disconsolate lad I made my way over to C Company and again did not see anybody I knew, except the company commander, Captain Hull, who I knew had joined the 6th Battalion as a second lieutenant in September 1939, when we were billeted in Lytton Street, Middlesbrough. It is he who wrote a book, *The Man from Alamein* by C. M. Hull and the story is fact. He was a very brave officer, having proved himself in France in 1939, and would go through hell for his company of men.

After being put into number Fifteen Platoon, I began getting to know the other lads and found out that my section leader was a young man named Lance Corporal Coughlan. I had tiffin (lunch) with them, then sat to one side, my brain in a turmoil, remembering all the old names and faces I had known since August 1939, but in the infantry one had to learn to come to terms with sudden death and changing circumstances and get on with life. I did just this and soon became involved in what we had to do, getting to know that most of the lads belonging to the new 6th were just as good soldiers as those I had known in the past.

While we were at the spot where I joined the company, the mobile showers came up and gave us a treat. Some of the lads said that it had been a month since they had seen a shower. The battalion was having a three-day rest before it moved forward to face more action. Orders came to move.

The Germans had fortified positions among the hills in Tunisia and we had to assault them. We enbussed and travelled a distance of about sixty miles. Abandoned

German guns and all sorts of paraphernalia of war were everywhere – but not as bad as Dunkirk. It was dark when we arrived at our destination and we found ourselves in more or less open ground, about five miles from the enemy-held hills. We rested here that day and prepared for battle, receiving details of the expected opposition and the situation in general, relating to our attack.

Within twenty-four hours we were told that we were going into action and to prepare ourselves.

Chapter 12

Wadi Akarit, Into Battle

IT WAS explained to us in detail that the enemy were dug in at a place called Wadi Akarit in Tunisia and 'had to be sent packing', to use General Montgomery's words. The code name for the forthcoming battle was Operation Scipio.

As the day dawned, we enbussed and were taken to a clearing about three miles away, which was screened from the enemy by trees. By now, it was getting dusk and we were assembled and told in great detail and in no uncertain terms what was expected of us; also the method to be used to dislodge the enemy. Great emphasis was placed upon our part, the 6th battalion. This was so different to the attitude of our commanders previously, when we faced the enemy without any knowledge of the part we had to play. Unlike years ago, we were treated not as a number, but as a human being, by our officers and the lads responded accordingly by showing more interest than had previously been the case, simply because we had been put in the picture. Our officers, too, showed greater enthusiasm for the conflict knowing that they had the confidence of those who were behind them in what was to be done.

The enemy were ensconced on hills in the distance, only four miles away, and the plan of attack was as follows. The enemy held a good, strong position overlooking our every move on the perfectly flat plain over which we were to advance. He had the advantage of looking down upon us from, on the left, Jebel Fatnassa (Jebel is the Arabic for hill) reaching a height of about 152m. On the right was Jebel Roumana, which was about the same height. These hills were joined by Hachana ridge.

Both hills were rather steep at the front, but our battalion was to attack a section just right of centre where the ground was level. Running through the valley was Wadi Akarit, an old dried-up riverbed. In the background, there was a range of hills which stretched as far as we could see and running along the length of the front of the lower ground was an anti-tank ditch about six feet deep and eight feet wide, the whole area being mined and barbed-wired. We were given all the necessary information relating to the attack and with strict instruction to, 'Give the buggers hell.'

The attack was to go in as follows: the 51st Highland Division on the right, the 4th Indian Ghurka Division on the left; our 69th Brigade would attack the centre gap, the 5th East Yorks on the left, the 7th Green Howards in the centre, and the 6th Green Howards on the right, but owing to the narrowness of the gap, the 6th would be in front of the 7th and would assault a prominent feature known as point 85, then we would spread out and let the 7th in.

We crossed the start line at 0400 hrs on a lovely moonlit night. It was difficult to believe we would soon be in the heat of the battle. It was almost eerie. Everything was so quiet at this early hour and then, all of a sudden, as if somebody had pressed a switch, everything came to life as our twenty-five pounders opened up and we moved forward at a steady walking pace. We were led by our officers onto the flat plain, devoid of trees, and kept a distance of four or five yards apart. Advancing at a steady walking pace towards our objective, we had gone about one mile when the enemy let us know that he was expecting us and was responding accordingly. Shells began to fall a little way in front of us, then behind us and amongst us. He had found the range with the result that some of our lads began to fall, wounded, killed, at times blown to smithereens. Then their mortars began to take their toll amongst us. By now, of course, our own artillery, the twenty-five pounders, began to fire and we could see the resulting explosions in the distance. Also at this time, our own guns were laying down a creeping barrage. This is a barrage of shells, which keeps moving just ahead of the infantry, and as we moved forward so did the barrage – until it was lifted. Sometimes, the barrage would fall too short, with unpleasant results.

The Sappers had gone in quietly during the night to make paths through the minefields, marking them with white tape. I was twenty-five years of age, but many of the boys around me were only nineteen and had never even heard of a twenty-five pounder and I don't know what they were thinking. In the early dawn, the enemy dropped Very lights from an aeroplane, making the dawn as light as day and showing up every detail clearly. It looked eerie and very soon we could hear the chatter of machine guns and felt that every bullet was aimed at us personally.

The enemy now opened up with 88mm and the shells were soon bursting amongst us with more accuracy as we advanced about eight yards apart, with our rifles across our chests. The enemy threw everything at us and we felt very exposed on that flat plain but there was no turning back. Hell, I felt vulnerable but never afraid – we had other things to think about! Strangely enough, at this stage, fear never entered our heads; the job had to be done and there was no turning back.

Two thousand yards from the gap there was not even the usual scrub to drop behind. The 69th Brigade soon ran into trouble. Our C Company made a very spirited attack on point 85 and took it with the loss of some good lads. The East Yorks and the 7th Battalion were pinned down by heavy frontal and enfilade machine gun fire (This is where weapons fire can be directed, for instance, on a column or row of troops such that the projectiles travel the length of the column or row). The 4th Indian and 51st Highland had been successful in their initial attacks and somewhat reduced the firing down onto us and we advanced cautiously.

As we got nearer to the enemy and could sense the height of Fatnassa and Roumana above us, the fire from their machine guns, mortars and 88s slackened off because we were below their line of fire, except for a time to the left of us. Up to now, tanks had not put in an appearance as they would have been very exposed on the flat ground and were waiting until the soldiers took the Jebels.

By the time we had reached the above-mentioned position, the Ghurkas had already gone into action in the dead of night in their usual way, stealthily, without any artillery support whatsoever, their Kukries (a very sharp, curved, broad knife about eighteen inches long) demanding a heavy penalty. These very brave soldiers from Nepal must have put the fear of death into the enemy. On the other hand, the enemy would not live long enough to be afraid, because in seconds his decapitated head would be on the ground.

Also during the dark hours, under cover of our twenty-five pounders, one tank had reached the anti-tank ditch and filled about ten yards of it in, sufficient for us to cross over. This tank had been knocked out and was still on top of the filled-in ditch and a very gory sight confronted us. The tank commander had been killed, I would say, by machine gun fire. His body, or what remained of it, was hanging over the edge of the turret. It had almost been cut in two. His head and shoulders were intact, but the whole middle of his body was splattered over the side – the intestines hanging out where the stomach had been ripped open. Blood flowed freely. The commander must have been standing in the hatch observing when the tank was hit. What an awful sight. How cheap life was. Many of our young lads had not been in action before and this was the sight which greeted them. I wonder what their thoughts were, because no matter what, this was war and our job had to be done. I passed within six feet of that tank and the hoards of flies were already at work. It was a good job that the tank commander's loved ones would never know how he had died – just 'killed in action' covered every eventuality in war.

We crossed the ditch and started to enter the foothills but were pinned down for a while, being overlooked from higher ground. The hills had slit trenches all over them so were good for defence and we could see nobody to fire back at. But eventually we managed to make some headway, keeping our bodies low and then separating into our individual sections, all the while being shelled, mortared and sniped, suffering casualties.

The Wadi Akarit – a dried-up riverbed – was about five thousand yards long, running inland from the sea. My section moved along the top of the Wadi, advancing further into the hills, then making for higher ground on the right of us, and shells were bursting all the time around us but happily not too near our section then suddenly we were fired upon from across the valley and one boy was killed as we froze to the ground. The slightest movement of our bodies brought fire to bear upon us for about twenty minutes until, quite unexpectedly, two of our tanks came along the bank of the Wadi and fired shell after shell on the machine gun post pinning us down. We then made our way to join more of our company down the hill in the Wadi, which was about thirty feet wide with almost straight sides four or five feet deep, just starting to crumble; I can easily recall having to jump down into it.

We were now attacking as platoons and sections, and our section, led by Lance Corporal Coughlan, bending low to the ground, moved to the right and we had to tread warily because we were very often overlooked. We must have advanced about two hundred yards, not realising that we were being observed from a concealed trench. All of a sudden machine gun fire came from our right and we dropped flat. We knew roughly where the fire came from, and quite unexpectedly Coughlan did a silly thing; without any command he stood up to move forward, instead of giving us instructions to fire while he observed. He was no sooner on his feet than a single shot rang out and Coughlan, who was next to me on my right, dropped dead in an instant. It was an awful experience seeing poor Coughlan's life being ended so suddenly.

For a moment, we could not believe it, then my rage was up and I, being the senior soldier, took command. It all happened in seconds and I shouted to the other lads to keep firing towards the enemy trench on the hillside to make them keep their heads down. Angry, I grabbed poor Coughlan's sub-machine gun and shouted: 'Come on lads, kill the bastards, send them to hell, but keep firing and don't forget your grenades.' Firing as I was running, I killed the first Italian who showed his head. When we were about ten yards away we had reached the top of the slit trench and we killed the survivors, five of them cowering in the bottom of the trench. It was no time for pussy footing; we were consumed with rage and had to kill them to pay for our fallen pal. We were so intoxicated; we could not hold back, given the chance they would have killed us. This much I had learned at Dunkirk – no quarter given – and those Italians paid the supreme penalty. It was almost impossible to believe that a healthy young man's life could be ended in a split second. Only a few minutes before, I was talking to Coughlan and now he was dead. That event is still imprinted in my thoughts as if it were yesterday.

There was no activity from the air to speak of. The fact is that our fighting was taking place amongst a range of hills and from the air it must have been impossible to distinguish friend from foe. Whatever the reason, we did not see a single aircraft.

Our divisional partners in the battle were holding their own in the attack and for a very short period there was a lull in firing and it was almost quiet. After so much gunfire it was suspected that a counter attack would be launched and that is just what happened. All of a sudden, the enemy opened up with 88s and mortars and we made haste to our various section positions, while our supporting artillery reacted to the enemy shelling. The 88s were proving to be a great hindrance to us but they always were; our battalion was held back a little while the 4th Indian and 51st Highland advanced further to threaten the enemy, and we moved forward.

Then we saw the enemy moving furtively across the hills. Letting them get a little closer, our officers shouted, 'Let them have it, lads!' We all jumped up, firing our weapons, as we had all lost pals and were as mad as hell. Our Bren gunner, a tough kid, was really on the boil and ran forward firing the Bren from the hip, with his Number Two changing magazines as they ran. They were awarded the Military Medal and sadly they were both later killed in Normandy.

A few of our lads fell wounded but the enemy attack was too inadequate to succeed (this was really no tank country so the enemy only used infantry against us) and our blood was up as we had all lost pals in the fighting, so we gave them bloody hell! It took another four hours of killing and winkling out the enemy from his trenches and filthy dugouts in the hillsides before the firing quietened down, then stopped. They did not take much persuading to put up their hands and be herded back behind us.

We went over the whole area which had been held by the enemy, finding caves which had been dug into the hillsides, and in many of them you could smell perfume and there was much evidence of females having been present. The Italians liked their comforts. Though we had heard about these things previously, it had been hard to believe, but now we knew. As we went about our work, some of our boys walked into an anti-personnel minefield and a few were wounded.

There was much clearing up to be done and the odd sniper to be dealt with, then the opportunity came to rest for an hour and a meal was brought up to us, which was always bully stew and boiled rice on these occasions and it was always good. Mess tins out, into the queue, and we were soon feeling replete, but not so much that we couldn't continue fighting. We just sat around, talking of the day and its happenings. There had been no rest since the early hours of the morning, so many of the lads lay on their backs smoking, trying to relax. Our company commander settled us all down and said he was very satisfied with the way we had conducted ourselves, which was typical of Captain Hull. We had lost many good soldiers, but it was not possible to escape from the things we had witnessed until we had to move on. Then we would accept that these killings were unavoidable. It would be fatal to dwell too much on what we had experienced.

Years later, I discovered that the Green Howards and East Yorkshires had killed or captured practically the whole of the Italian Spezia Division. Our casualties in the 6th were several officers killed and wounded together with one hundred and twenty ranks. It had been a sad day and we welcomed a few days' rest to lick our wounds.

After the meal, another boy and I were detailed to go and bury one of our lads who had been killed (it was too hot to leave bodies lying around and the stretcher bearers were busy taking care of the wounded) so off we went with our entrenching tools.

Although I had seen a good many dead soldiers, I had never been called upon to bury one. Unfortunately, there was no body as such, but only the gruesome remains. It had been blown to pieces. The legs and one arm were lying yards away, there was no face and the body was ripped apart. Never before had I seen anything like it and I found it very difficult to contain myself. We dug a shallow grave in the stony ground and put the torn limbs into it, then I found the identity discs and, to my horror, I found the dead boy to be Arthur Oxley, one of my pals on the *Queen Mary*. We looked around for any other things belonging to Arthur and found half of a Green Howard cap badge. It was twisted by the blast and I still have it as a memory of my pal. I don't know how I contained my emotions at that moment. Together, we made a cairn of stones on the grave, hoping that it would be found, though it was such a lonely hillside, I did not think it would be discovered. We left one identity disc with the body, the other we took back to our officer to whom we explained what we had done.

How strange it was that despite the trauma of such events these things were, of necessity, put to the back of my mind. We could not allow ourselves to be influenced unduly. It was time to move on. The enemy had fled, leaving many bodies and weapons lying around. It had been one hell of an experience. On our way through the low hills, we finally ended up on level ground and the first thing we saw was a battery of abandoned 88mm guns. It was the first time I had seen that powerful weapon, which was so much talked about, and which played havoc amongst us. We could not go too near them in case they had been booby-trapped or the Germans had left mines around.

All next day I could not forget how a human body could be so violated as was Arthur Oxley's. I was certain the body would not be found but nevertheless I later wrote to the War Graves Commission and was informed that the body had been recovered and buried in Grave no 26, Plot 2, Row D at the Sfax war cemetery in Tunisia.

We now rested, guards posted forward, and it was soon dark. Then we slept where we were, on the ground, our heads on our packs. This sad day was over and it was said that the battle of Wadi Akarit was one of the most successful fought by the Eighth Army. Our company commander won the MC. The 8th Armoured Brigade, followed by the New Zealand Division, now passed through our lines and continued to pursue and harass the enemy on his retreat to Tunis.

Next morning, we walked only about five miles and were halted for two days. The 5th East Yorkshires had also come to rest next to us, so I went over to see if I could find John Bousfield, who had been my best pal on the *Queen Mary*, only to be told he had been killed by one of our twenty-five pounder shells, which had fallen short during the creeping barrage. It was a bitter blow to me. It was almost impossible to believe that both Arthur and John, two grand young lads, had been killed when only a very short time ago we had been laughing and joking. John was only nineteen years of age; his parents had the Turk's Head Hotel in Stockton. It was a stark reminder that under the circumstances in which we lived our life was of little significance and we had to live from day-to-day. It would not have been healthy for us to dwell on whatever emotions we could have given way to, but they were such days of sadness.

Being an infantryman was indeed a demanding life with many hurdles, which we had to adapt ourselves to overcome. Sometimes it was a trial of strength between our head and our heart, but common sense and duty usually prevailed and yesterday's happenings were put to the back of our thoughts until sometime in the future. What a tragedy war is. Amongst the many other casualties at Wadi Akarit were Sergeant Myson, Corporal Smith, the company commander's batman and Regimental Sergeant Major Carter. I will never forget 6 April 1943 and every year, on that date, I think about Wadi Akarit.

Chapter 13

Preparing

WE HAD taken up positions in countryside, along a ridge, where we were in company with palm trees and some undergrowth. We were near a village called Enfidaville, which was about two miles to our right. The 8th Armoured Brigade, followed by the New Zealand Division, now passed through our lines and continued to pursue the enemy on his retreat.

Rommel had made a stand just north of Enfidaville, and our 69th Brigade went to relieve the Guards' Brigade in reserve position in some olive groves about one thousand yards south of Enfidaville. Later in the day, we went through the town and took up positions just north of the main road. We were now off the order of battle for three days to rest. Nothing would be more welcome than to lie in a grass field and rest our heads on our small packs, and that is just what we did.

Two days later, the main attack took place by the New Zealand and 4th Indian Divisions supported by the Guards' Brigade. The enemy were soon retreating northwards and our front quietened down, with the exception of the odd 88mm shell landing in our area, but it was nothing to cause us any anxiety and the sound of our twenty-five pounder shells screaming overhead was music to our ears. They were giving Jerry a pasting! It would be springtime in England, very much like Tunisia in April, the difference being that it was hot during the day and very cold at night.

Tunisia, unlike many Arab countries, is green and mostly fertile, and as we passed through the countryside it was a treat to see oranges, lemons, bananas and date palms growing. There were fewer flies than everywhere else too, but mosquitoes plagued us and any uncovered part of our bodies was a target for them. I had nineteen bites on one hand. Many of the lads suffered from malaria at a later date, but it seems the Mepacrine tablets we were given worked for me.

Shortly, out of the blue, came a welcome surprise. The mail had caught up with us and I received seven letters. It was the first mail I had received since leaving home and I was delighted. It was a most pleasant feeling to think that those letters had come from England. Amidst all the turmoil of war, the mail had managed to get through. Everybody was so pleased. I read those letters repeatedly, scrutinising every word for weeks, in fact, until the next mail arrived, quite some time after.

We cleaned weapons and awaited more reinforcements to replace the lads lost in the battle. Much warlike activity was taking place ahead of us and the enemy was being very hard pressed, but we were not included in the action. Our division did not see any further part in this theatre of war. The honour of seeing the enemy routed right out of North Africa was largely being left to others who had not already chased the enemy for two thousand miles. And 50th Division would not be able to relish the opportunity of seeing the total surrender in Tunisia of an enemy who had put up such tenacious resistance from Alamein (Egypt) to Enfidaville (Tunisia); a pity, because I think we would have enjoyed seeing the Afrika Korps surrender. This was also the case in Sicily and Europe – first to land but withdrawn at Letojanni (before the end at Messina) to train for D-Day; first on our front to land on D-Day then withdrawn near Arnhem because of lack of reinforcements, before the end in Germany – and it was not playing the game! And now the Americans, who had had some minor skirmishes with the Germans, since they landed, had to take the glory. I console myself with the fact that 50th Division was always withdrawn for more important roles, so that at least is something to be proud of. It gave a chap a tremendous feeling to think he was part of the Eighth Army.

Nobody knew why we had been taken out of action. I suppose, at the time, none of us cared either, expecting that the high command would have the situation well in hand. This was by no means always the way we thought!

On 14 April 1943, or thereabouts, a fleet of three-tonners turned up in our motor transport compound and next day we were enlightened a little more. We had to pack our kit and we enbussed. Our convoy began its journey at just a steady speed. Any ex-serviceman will know that army vehicles had governors – a device to prevent speeding – on the engine. And because of the concentration of armour, and much else on the roads, it took us three days to reach an area just north of Sousse. After resting for tiffin, we took to the road again and camped a few miles north of Sfax, on the coast. After another two days' rest, we were on the move again. It was about 23 April.

What lay ahead of us, nobody knew, but we were most surprised to learn that we were going by road back to Egypt, a journey of about two thousand miles taken in easy stages to minimise wear and tear on the vehicles, especially for the benefit of those conscientious chaps of the Royal Army Service Corps (RASC), whom I don't believe ever received the credit they deserved for the demanding work they did during the war years.

So, we were going back to the flies, but that was of no importance after what we had experienced over the past few days. We were going to retrace the steps of the many soldiers who had fought in battles, back and forth, all the way to the Delta of Egypt. What a gruesome story these sands could tell about the many young lives that had been sacrificed. It had been a very traumatic time in my life, going over the action in my mind, thinking of every detail. Poor Arthur Oxley and the tank commander, whose bodies had been so violated dominated my thoughts; their loved ones would not yet know of their deaths. Thank goodness they would never know how they died. I wondered if the shattered remains of soldiers were ever found. Even if they weren't, their souls were at rest with their maker and what remained would crumble into dust where he had buried them.

I said a little prayer to myself as we passed Akarit. My religious thoughts were most important to me. I imagined the faces of the pals I had lost and could see them just as they were before they gave their lives. The paraphernalia of war lay everywhere; destroyed, burnt or abandoned. Only the dead bodies had gone. But now in Tunisia, the Germans were getting all they deserved.

Every two years, for many years, I have looked through my wartime souvenirs and read my memoirs. Perhaps I am a sentimental old fool, but comradeship was ingrained into my character for seven years and will be part of my memories for as long as I live. I sincerely hope that never again will our country be caught napping the same as they were in 1939. Around ten miles past Wadi Akarit, our convoy halted. It was going to be an eleven-day journey, so every day at around 1700 hrs we laid up. Now we were in a large, green field, which sloped slightly. I can recall sitting down a little way from a hedgerow; we would be kipping down beneath the stars. Our company commander, Captain Hull, was wandering among the lads, talking about nothing in particular. He was closer and more popular with the lads than he had ever been, having shared the same experiences with them. He knew full well what comradeship was all about. Remembering him from the autumn of 1939 he was so different. Now he was a man's man and he realised it, which was good. He was infatuated with the art of war. Just as Captain Hull had respect for our officers, we stood up as he approached us, ignoring the fact that he had told us to remain where we were.

He knew full well who I was because he knew I had been company commander's batman some time earlier and he spoke to me, asking about how Lance Corporal Coughlan had died, since he had known the lad when he was in the battalion intelligence section. Then he surprised me by saying: 'By the way, Cheall, I am told that you used to do a little cooking back in the 11th Battalion.' I replied, 'That's right, Sir'. He wanted to know if I would fancy trying my hand at being company officer's cook, so I asked if the same particular arrangement would apply and would I be cooking only when our company was separated from other companies so that at all other times I would be mucking in with the lads. When we were in action, the officers ate the same as the men and I'm sure that is one of the reasons we had such respect for our officers. They showed no sign of superiority and spoke to us in our language. So I kept in touch with the lads and also improved my knowledge of cooking, hoping I had not taken too much on, because cooking in the field is far removed from cooking in the cookhouse. No sooner had I volunteered than a second lieutenant walked up to me and said, 'Right, Cheall, what's for dinner?' Of course, he was only kidding then, though I did return to where I had been resting and thought about what I had taken on.

Before we settled down to sleep, we looked around and could imagine we were in England; the stars were flickering in the sky and the moon was shining. Who would believe that so very recently war had passed this way? Phantom figures moved across the field, making their way hither and thither on duty and I could make out the guards watching over the vehicles. Apart from the moon, it was dark because we were out of range of the cacophony of war. These were the moments when our thoughts might turn to home before we went to sleep.

It was 0500 hrs when I was awakened by the guard and after splashing water on my face I made my way to the field kitchen the company cooks had set up. I needed to draw some rations, so that I could prepare breakfast for the five C Company officers. They were a grand lot in the army. The sergeant cook said, 'Well, Cheall, what are you after?' At first he thought I was having him on, so he said 'Bugger off, grub's up in two hours,' and insisted that I was 'coming the old soldier', as the army saying goes. Eventually, I was given the rations when my platoon commander came up and explained.

Fortunately, I had prepared my cooking stove yesterday evening. It was an unorthodox cooking arrangement but one which all desert soldiers knew about. It was not an easy task, as many a time the only fire I had was by filling a jam jar with sand, soaking it with petrol then lighting it. We also washed our clothes in petrol. On this occasion, I cut a water can into two halves (we had square water cans in those days) filled them with sand and soaked it with petrol, added a match and I had a fire, very primitive, but effective. The result of my efforts seemed to impress my officers; basically, it was the same food as the lads, but served up more individually with care. I am not implying criticism of the company cooks, who usually did an excellent job, but they were providing food for a lot of hungry young men who certainly did not care how it was served up as long as it was plentiful, and certainly at that stage of the war we never went hungry.

Continuing on our way next morning, we left behind the green country of Tunisia and entered Libya where we were back in the inhospitable desert. The convoy stopped for quick tiffin and a brew-up after we had passed through Tripoli, which was a hive of activity in order to get the post working.

It had only taken six months for our army to chase the enemy from Alamein to Tunisia, with many rearguard actions being fought in the process. Libya was not a very attractive country in those days; sand, sand and more sand, which we would have to get used to until we reached the Egyptian Delta. We would not see much else apart from the debris of war which littered the ground everywhere. The Arabs must have had a whale of a time when a battle had moved on.

It had been a very hot, sunny day, which developed into a night when the sky seemed full of stars. The flies were still a plague as they had been at Qassasin camp.

For mile after mile, the sandscape seemed endless, as did the coast road. We were covered in yellow dust and although we only had on a shirt and shorts we sweated profusely beneath the blazing sun. It had been a month since we had been able to have a shower, or even a good wash.

During the afternoon, we stopped about five miles south of Benghazi, where a meal was brought up to us and we were able to stretch our legs; that was until, on the horizon, it looked foggy. That fog was a sand storm (a Khamseen) approaching us; we just had time to jump into our trucks and fasten the flaps down when it hit us. It lasted about forty-five minutes, during which time there was almost nil visibility and when it had passed, sand was piled up against the truck and there was sand in everything. It was just south of this area that the 150th Brigade of 50th Division had been annihilated in January, almost all being killed or captured. We stayed the night near Benghazi, which had been occupied alternately by both combatants during the conflict. It was called the 'Benghazi handicap', because of the opposing forces going back and forth.

Our convoy was travelling along the coast road, through day-after-day of scorching sun. This road had certainly witnessed a tremendous amount of military traffic over the past two years. The Afrika Korps, the Eighth Army and the Italians had all advanced then fled along it, as the fighting fluctuated, leaving behind them enormous quantities of the debris of war as evidence of their passage. I bet the Germans went hell for leather when the Eighth Army was chasing them. Passing south of Tobruk, I thought of the stubborn resistance which had been shown by the British and Empire soldiers in their effort to deny the port to Rommel.

Our long journey was over. It would be about 6 May 1943 when we reached our destination. Our home for the next five weeks was a camp called Sidi Bishr, which was not too far from Alexandria. The camp itself was a hard, sandy and sparse grassy field which was covered by mostly small tents, each to be occupied by three soldiers who had to be on their knees to crawl in – not much fun. It was just to the side of the main road to Alexandria and each battalion had its own area. A couple of us were sitting having a mess tin of tea and we wondered if any thought had even been given to how many lives had been sacrificed by the navies, armies and air forces of the combatants. From Malta, across the Mediterranean to Tunisia, and for over two thousand miles along the coast of North Africa, battles had been fought to keep the enemy from getting his hands on the oil of the Middle East. It was a sad reflection upon the ill preparedness of our country for war, because if in 1939 we had been as prepared as the Germans for what was about to engulf us, the war would not have lasted so long. The British Tommy was at least as good as, if not better than, any soldier in the world. There was no doubt about his ability to beat the enemy as soon as the comparable weapons were made available.

At this camp we only did the usual inspection of kits and rifles. There were very few parades. It was really a kind of holiday. After a certain amount of organisation, one platoon at a time from each company was given a three-day pass to go to Alexandria (We could also go in for a few hours at a time). The local buses ran along the road very near to the camp. My pal, George Bertram, and I went on leave together and found a place in a street which ran parallel behind the wide promenade sea front. It was only like a boarding house; if anything, more spartan. A swarthy owner sat at a desk just inside the door where we paid our piastres and were given a key and room number. It was a very plain room with a thin carpet, hard bed, two chairs and a table with a water jug and bowl on it. Who cared? We didn't. Remember, money was not plentiful so we had to be careful with it. We had to go to the YMCA for meals and cakes and a good cup of tea.

While we were out one day a lad from the East Yorks called to see me and he went into my room and, seeing some cream cakes, took a fancy to them. I had bought them from the YMCA. Just a small memory, but he left a note saying he was sorry he had missed us and I still have that letter. Charlie Lee, who came from Yorkshire, was killed in Sicily.

While I was in Alexandria, I thought I would go down to the docks to see if, by any chance, HMS *York*, a cruiser, happened to be there because I knew it was in the Mediterranean. The reason for my interest was that before the war I had a good pal called Bill Collings, who had become an engine room artificer on board *York*. I went to the gate, explained, and showed my pay book, and the chap informed me that the ship had been damaged in action but had managed to reach Suda Bay, in Crete. Whilst undergoing repairs, an Italian remote controlled explosive motorboat had hit her during the battle for Crete. Although the ship sank, only two lads lost their lives and Bill was one of them. What made this fact much worse was that Bill Collings had a younger brother, Vernon, who was in the RAF and when he was stationed in India, had picked up a bug. The lad was rushed back to Glasgow where he died. What a tragedy for their parents. The boys were aged nineteen and twenty-one. When my wife and I used to visit their parents after the war, Mrs Collings in particular had never got over losing her two sons.

Alexandria was a very busy place, with people of all creeds crowding the streets. The trams were outrageous, simply loaded with people. They seemed to be clinging on to everything except the wheels, just like flies round a jam pot. I never found out if anybody paid a fare! One thing I do remember, though, is that each morning when I went out – I kept myself fairly smart in my khaki drill – there were photographers about waiting for anybody in uniform. I still have the snaps, which I treasure. It was OK and a change from the routine, but we never had sufficient money.

The small boot boys, garbed in their kaftans, amused me. One of them, in particular, looked a little imp. He came to me and he would say: 'Hey sojer, I clean you boots, I clean good and shiny.' Well, he was such a little character, about nine or ten years of age and pitch black with white teeth, so this 'sojer' let him do his cleaning each morning, even though my boots were already as shiny as they possibly could be.

There was one thing that many of the lads went to Alexandria for. Well, any serviceman who was going into the city was told to be aware of loose women, and the place to go for you-know-what was the official place. I think all the married men and many of the young lads soon found their way there. It was called Sister Street. Out of sheer curiosity, we just had to go and have a look at the place. And no, I didn't! I could not accept that it was morally justified or sensible having sex with a female of dubious nationality when hundreds and thousands of all kinds of men were at the same game.

It had been an eye opener to see Alexandria and get to know how these people from the Middle East behaved. Our three days had been a complete change and most certainly a rest for us. As we made our way back to camp, our thoughts turned to other things and the real reason for being in the Middle East. We knew that there was something in the wind, to bring us all the way from Tunisia to the Delta and we could only imagine what lay ahead of us.

The day after we arrived in camp, the whole battalion had to parade, to be taken to a hospital where we each had to give a pint of blood. It was the first time I had given blood, any of us for that matter. We were all young and very fit and our young English blood would certainly have improved the blood bank stocks. Oh, to be virile and fit, it was a great feeling; sad that so many of the lads were to die in the not too distant future.

Suddenly, I thought about the misfortunes of the 6th Battalion since they had arrived in the Middle East, during June 1941. I could not believe it was only six weeks since I had joined them at Tripoli and still had not recognised more than ten of the old 6th Battalion. The remainder must have been killed or captured in action. Even *The Story of the Green Howards* by Thackeray Synge does not tell me about such large losses and the details of what had become of one thousand soldiers are very vague. The few I had come across did not seem to want to talk about their experiences of the past two years.

We soon returned to the old routine and taking care of our weapons was of supreme importance. However, we didn't settle down for long because in two days we were on the move again. From Sidi Bishr, we moved through Cairo to alongside the Suez Canal for intensive training. During this trip, I saw the Pyramids and Sphinx.

We arrived at Kabrit, a very desolate camp near the southern end of the Suez Canal, on the edge of the Sinai dessert on the shores of the Bitter Lakes, and not far from the Red Sea. A week's intensive training awaited us, but for a different method of tactics to any we had yet undertaken. The only inhabitants we saw there were the usual scrounging Arabs with their filthy camels. It was laughable, upon reflection. We used to make our tea then dry out the leaves in the sun then sell the tea to the Arabs. What a fiddle – but why not? These were the same kind who would descend on a battlefield, after the fighting was over, and they would be like vultures, stripping bodies and machines of anything valuable.

The training was hard at Kabrit and on one occasion we did a march of thirty miles along the Suez Canal in intense heat to a camp near some oil refineries. On one occasion, we were transported to the Gulf of Akaba. We boarded a landing craft and were then taken about two miles down the Gulf. Turning around, we made a dash for the coast at a good speed and when we were about one hundred yards from the beach the ramp crashed down and, simulating the real thing, we jumped into waist deep water and went as fast as we could, encouraged by our NCOs. As we were laden with all kit and weapons, it was a little difficult to keep our feet. We charged up the beach shouting wildly, and firing blank ammunition at an imaginary enemy. We would have been sitting ducks in that case. I realise that this is 'old hat' now but in those days it was all new to us. It was strenuous, but easy; there were no enemies firing at us and we could imagine from past experience what it would be like under real conditions.

Later in the day, during a mess tin of char, we were all talking and realized that we were going to invade somewhere but, of course, how could we know where at that time? Everything had to be so secret. We did a lot of other training to make us fitter than we had ever been; laden with kit we would run up and down sand hills to strengthen our legs and jump into fifteen-feet-deep sand pits. Included in the training were two thirty-mile route marches along the Suez Canal. The heat was intense and the flies plagued us. We now knew why we had been taken off the order of battle at Enfidaville and 50th Division was going to be taking an active part in whatever was being planned. I feel sure the lads were never fitter than we were at that time.

Back in camp at Kabrit, the restriction on mail was lifted for a while so I sent home all my photographs and letters I wanted to keep, in case anything happened to me (for that same reason, I had put my name and number on the back of them). All written mail was censored, though who would want to worry our loved ones by telling them of our experiences? It was strange, but the possibility that we might never return to England didn't enter our minds, which was just as well.

Eventually, we were told what was planned for us – our 50th Division was to take part in the invasion of Sicily.

Chapter 14

Sicily

OUR TRAINING for what lay ahead of us was now complete, and we embarked at Suez on the *Tegelburg* and sailed through the Suez Canal to Port Said, where we boarded HMT *Orontes*. As the convoy assembled, we knew that this was going to be a very large operation. We had never before seen so many ships together. We were told there were over three thousand vessels taking part in the largest amphibious invasion ever undertaken.

Our imagination ran wild with the prospect, since it was still enshrouded in mystery, and there was a great deal of speculation. We set sail on 5 July 1943 and there was quite a swell going and we hoped it was not going to be too rough. The ship's tannoy suddenly came to life to give us the information we were anxious to hear. It was to be Sicily and the operation was to be code-named Husky.

We had never taken part in an invasion and our minds boggled at the prospect but we were not at all apprehensive about the task which we were to undertake. We were told all we needed to know for the job we had to do, including the landing place, what the whole invasion force consisted of and also what was expected of us during the operation.

In the distance, we could see Mount Etna against the horizon on the port side, with that red ball of sun sinking into the sea. On this occasion 69th Brigade, which comprised of the 5th East Yorks and 6th and 7th Green Howards, was to be the follow-up to the initial assault and we would be landing at Avola, which was south of Syracuse on the southeast corner of the island. It was around midnight on 10 July when the anchor went down with a rumble. We were about seven miles from the enemy coast, time seemed to be stood still and we waited and waited for the signal to go.

During the early hours, around 0430 hrs, the waiting was over and we moved towards the side of the ship, then over we went, heavily laden. Seeking a foothold on the scrambling nets was something which we had never rehearsed and I must admit that it was a bit daunting. The assault craft were bobbing up and down like corks and it was a strange sensation to go to put our foot on something solid and finding it wasn't solid at all, but almost alive.

In those days, most of us could not swim, though we were not short of confidence. But the usual flow of banter among the lads vanished for a while – though there was no shortage of swear words when one of the lads missed a foothold. By the time the other assault craft were ready and in line, abreast, it would be about 0600 hrs; it was fine, but there was a heavy sky and a fair swell was running; we were on our way.

The sector of the beach designated for 69th Brigade to assault had code name 'Jig' and was near to Avola, and we were due to land at 0800 hrs but apart from the odd shell our own battalion was not expecting much enemy fire, since other Green Howards, the 7th Battalion, would go in before us. Their first objective was to be Syracuse but they did not encounter the resistance which had been expected. The slight opposition we came across, which had been bypassed by the leading units, was soon overcome, the enemy being taken prisoner and escorted to the rear. There was an airborne brigade to go in first but tragically many of their planes landed in the sea or in the mountains.

I know everybody was surprised at the lack of opposition, even though we had not been in the first wave, and consequently we were soon established on dry land, but with very wet legs, and a march of twenty miles was necessary before we reached a defensive position. By this time, we were feeling the effect of the lack of sleep whilst we had been aboard ship, the conditions being very cramped, plus the fact that the weather was hot and very humid; so very different to the weather in Africa where it was hot and dry.

At this point I was asked, once again, to take up the job of officers' cook – well, variety is the spice of life – though I didn't take up the job for some days as we were still on the move.

The best possible use was made of the position we found ourselves in and forward patrols were sent out probing the enemy and we achieved a modicum of sleep. Next morning, we progressed up the eastern side of the island to make an attack on Sortino and during our advance we encountered stiff opposition at certain strong points and a number of our men were killed, among them Sergeant Harrington and John Ryan. My pal, Charlie Lee, was missing. Jack Ramsden and all his section were blown to pieces. Jack Betley was also killed. The 7th Green Howards were also having a rough time. We constantly had to be aware of booby traps and hadn't to touch any civilian property because of the lethal traps the Germans had left behind.

I vividly recall patrolling along a railway line which ran through a massive lemon grove. When we came to search some buildings we found four naked bodies. Rigor mortis was complete and they were on their backs on a large bench. The bodies were black and were starting to decompose. They were being eaten by maggots and showed signs of having been tortured. I hoped the perpetrators suffered the wrath of God. During war, one sees many things and forgets but it has to be like that. We were soldiers, but I can still, after these many years, remember the bodies lying in that hut.

Sicily is a mountainous and beautiful island, lush green and hot, and the majestic, unpredictable Mount Etna could always be seen. We worked our way through the hills around Sortino and Lentini. We passed through olive, orange and lemon groves and miles of low tomato plants, more like small bushes than tomatoes, with those oval ones you see on cans in shops. And there was mile-upon-mile of seedless grapes. We walked through bushes laden with the fruit and would just grab a handful as we walked past. It was a delightful climate. Why did good, young lads have to be killed?

After we had cleared the villages of the enemy, the civilians appeared to welcome us, handing us fruit. They didn't have much else, and they wanted to show their appreciation to us for liberating their beloved country from the Germans.

Good roads were few and far between, almost all being comprised of compressed dirt, and whenever we had the opportunity to use transport great clouds of dust, particularly from the Bren carriers, were created along the winding roads around the mountains from which we had spectacular views down into the villages. Unfortunately, we were not there to admire the scenery but to kill or be killed. The enemy were making their way northwards leaving small, rear parties to hold us up as long as possible. They were easily disposed of, but it was very time-consuming having to dislodge them, and the enemy was retreating faster than we could advance. One of the roads we had to use was cut out of sheer rock overlooking the sea, about three hundred feet down below on the right, whilst the shear mountainside towered above us on our left. The enemy had blown the roads, leaving a gap of about ten yards and the Royal Engineers soon came forward and in record time placed a Bailey bridge across it and we were on our way again; those engineers certainly knew their job.

After we had progressed beyond the blown road, for the first time since our landing at Avola, the Germans were putting up a stiff resistance. This was going to be a larger operation and would involve the use of paratroops of both sides in the conflict. The problem was Primosole Bridge which spanned the River Simeto. It was holding up the advance and the Germans were as determined to hold it as our forces were take it. An airborne brigade was going to be dropped to take the bridge, which was seventeen miles ahead.

Leading the way as part of our 50th Division was the 151st Brigade of the Durham Light Infantry (It consisted of the 6th, 8th and 9th). These lads had a tremendous reputation for putting up a good fight and they were determined to uphold that record during the battle, which lasted for three days. At this stage, our 69th Brigade was in a position on the hillsides overlooking Primosole Bridge, though we were actually some distance away looking across the valley through which the river ran. Although not taking part in the actual attack, our battalion was being machine-gunned, shelled and mortared, causing many casualties amongst us. It is a surreal feeling being shelled and mortared.

In the first place, we had to assault these hills, denying them to the enemy for observation purposes. In the process we took thirty-five prisoners – Italian and

German – but unfortunately, we lost ten of our own men also. German prisoners were so different from Italians. The latter seemed pleased to be captured because at least they were alive, and although some Germans showed the same relief, others could have killed us with their arrogant looks. However, I can only write of what I know about because I saw it happen. This is in no way a military history, but back in 1943 I saw that both sides in the conflict used paratroops and the battle was fierce. After the killing was over, we were ordered to advance once again and only then realised just how bitter and stubborn the fighting had been. The whole area around the bridge was littered with dead bodies and all kinds of weapons and equipment. The bodies of these brave young soldiers were sprawled in pitiful positions, many floating in the water and some still visible lying on the riverbed, weighed down with gear, their parachutes floating on the water. The results of battle are not pleasant to witness and never forgotten by the survivors. War is evil, with the soldiers at the sharp end paying the highest price. Life is soon erased but memories linger on until, in time, the survivors join their comrades long gone. Having taken the bridge, we had a day's rest, but were being fired on at the same time.

During the period 18-21 July, our brigades were constantly attacking enemy positions in battles which are too numerous for me to detail. At midnight on the third day, the 6th Durham Light Infantry relieved us. Then General Montgomery decided that the 5th Division on our left should take up the attack. This division included the 1st Battalion Green Howards. In our rest positions, over the next four days, we were continually fired upon, but we were on the coast and were able to do a spot of bathing in the sea and generally have a rest. We received fifty new reinforcements.

On 25 July, we relieved the 8th Durham Light Infantry on the line and our regimental aid post was hit by shellfire. Captain Herbert, the Medical Officer, Captain Wallace, the Padre, and Private Wilson were killed. We were mortared here and Lieutenant Jackson and his batman were killed by a landmine. Starting to advance again, we were continually held up because of mines being laid indiscriminately by the enemy.

Once again, we came up against opposition to our progress. In the distance, Mount Etna looked down upon us, but in front of us was a very determined opposition by the enemy, deciding to make a stand at Catania airfield, which was well-defended and was not going to be subjugated easily. This was the airfield from which so many attacks upon Malta and our Royal Navy took place. During the hours of darkness, we made our advance and proceeded to dig deep slit trenches, since the whole area was in full view of the enemy who were observing from the hills about one mile away. Consequently, we were rather heavily shelled and mortared and suffered casualties. We kept in these positions for two days, and were very uncomfortable. Supplies came up to us during the hours of darkness.

Our officers left us to attend O groups (Orders) and upon returning told us what had taken place and what was planned to dislodge the enemy. Suddenly, our twenty-five pounders opened up with a tremendous barrage and the scream of the shells passing overhead was music to our ears. We could also hear the rumble of our tanks coming from the rear of us and this was our cue to advance in the usual way, in line abreast, under the orders of our platoon commander. Then we too came under fire from the enemy, with the result that some of our lads were killed or wounded.

The outcome of our attack was that the enemy relatively quickly evacuated his position, resulting in many Italian and German prisoners being taken, the Germans again making sure that it was their own kind who escaped to fight another day (almost always it was the Germans who took the transport and cleared out). Sicily was not tank country and the dirty roads were totally inadequate. It was also very mountainous and ideal for rearguard action by the enemy.

Soon after the action at Catania, we were resting overnight in a field (we had slept under the stars since the start of the invasion, never taking our clothes off, only our boots, sometimes putting our hot feet in a cold stream; it was heaven). Anyway, this particular night after we had laid up, some of our own tanks appeared in the field just over the hedge. After a short while, we heard gunfire not far from us. What had happened was that a tank crew member had been looking into the barrel of a gun, as we did when cleaning our rifles, and somehow or other the gun had fired and the soldier's head had been blown off and there, on the ground, was a headless and shoulderless body. What an awful way to die.

Once again, we were on foot and walking warily through villages of which there were many and which the enemy had recently occupied. We had to be extra vigilant because of snipers and booby traps, a game at which the Germans were proven experts. As we were making our way down a road, making sure that no enemy had been left behind to harass us, I saw a boy of about ten blown up into the air and killed after he had trodden on a mine concealed in the road. It was heartbreaking.

On about 17 August we heard that the Sicilian war was at an end. We were also told that although it had been a relatively short but fierce campaign, our 50th Division had played a very important part. Once again, Jerry was on the run; he was no longer master of all he surveyed.

On the march again, we eventually reached Letojanni, right on the coast. I remember walking with the other lads of our company and seeing the signpost to Letojanni. The seaside village was only half-a-mile away and that is where we were to rest our weary bodies and bathe in the sea and hope that mail would catch up with us. I had no idea that this was the end of the road for our battalion, although some units of 50th Division had gone as far as Messina and linked up with Americans. This day was 25 August 1943, my twenty-sixth birthday. It had seemed an age since I was called up in 1939 and I had survived many emotions. But this was just another day in the cycle of my life.

Battalion headquarters were billeted in Taormina, a lovely town so I am told, perched high above our village on the mountaintop. We were about forty miles from Messina.

The other lads of the company were now resting and making the most of being able to go into the sea, which they thoroughly deserved. Whilst there was some relaxation in discipline, I was informed that I would once again be taking up my duties as company officers' cook. Each company was in separate quarters, scattered along the coast; one at Catania and another at Syracuse. My free time was going to be very limited and I would miss every attitude of the lads and even their swearing. We were not by any stretch of the imagination wearing halos.

For the first time since landing we had a roof over our heads. Our officers occupied a house next to ours which was a property in which the batman and I lived. Our room was on the first floor and we slept on palliasses. On the ground floor was a well-equipped kitchen. The batman used to come down and have a chat with me. The officers also always knew where they could get a good cuppa, asking, 'Any tea, Cheall?' when they felt the need!

We had only been here a few days when the catering officer popped his head round the door to have a few words with me. Apparently, battalion HQ were having some very important visitors for a conference to be held there, during which time a meal was to be provided and not just opening a few tins of bully beef or ready-meal or even stewed rice. It was to be special. Apart from the headquarters' cooks, each company officers' cook had to make a contribution, so was I in the position of preparing a selection of hors d'oeuvres? I said that although I had never done so before I would have a crack at it. I was not lacking confidence. It so happened that I had in my kit a Mrs Beeton's cookery book which belonged to my sister. That is how I learned some of the finer points of cooking in the first place.

To prepare such delicacies off the top of my head would have been beyond my capabilities and there were some special supplies which I needed which would certainly not be available from the quartermaster at HQ. I spoke of my dilemma to my officer and within the hour the commanding officer's Jeep and driver turned up. 'Come on, Bill we are going for rations, to Messina.' The drive to the north-eastern corner of Sicily was a memorable experience. Driving like the wind in an open Jeep through the foothills of Etna was exhilarating, making me forget at least for a while the killing I had seen. It was a lovely journey because the road was clear of the enemy, as leading troops of 51st Division had already entered Messina. Passing through huge areas of oranges, lemons, olives, grapes, melons and even bananas made me wish I'd had a camera to record this treasured interlude.

Well, I stayed up almost all that night doing my share of the preparation of the meal, and it was a great success. Afterwards, when my officer came to see me, he told me that our battalion HQ had been the hosts to none other than General

Montgomery and General Eisenhower. I felt really chuffed and would never forget the occasion. It was quite an honour for me!

We were at Letojanni for about six weeks, during which time we expected each day to be on the move to invade Italy, but it almost seemed that we had been forgotten and our bodies would soon be losing their fitness because, apart from exercises on the beach, no energetic training had been undertaken to help us maintain the standard of fitness we had achieved by the end of the campaign. A punishing schedule had been maintained since we had returned to Egypt from Tunisia and it would be a pity to let ourselves relax too much after the strenuous effort we had made to chase the enemy from Sicily. The time would come when once again strenuous efforts would be needed to return to a peak of fitness.

My own time was taken up cooking three meals a day plus afternoon tea for our officers, though it did not keep me physically fit. When the time came for me to once again join the company, I paid the penalty by having to regain my former fitness. I can't recall what the lads did in their spare time, but I do know there was no entertainment whatsoever and nothing to drink other than water and the dreadful local drink, vino, which was like drinking vinegar. The local people were very few and the women seemed to have vanished. I wonder why!

I think there must have been a danger of the lads becoming bored. But little did we know that we were going to be among the first assault troops in the invasion of Europe.

Around 14 October 1943, we were ordered to start preparing for a move, but no destination had been mentioned. Our billets had to be cleaned out thoroughly so that an example of our disciplines could be demonstrated to the populace when they returned to their homes.

Our battalion was occupied in cleaning-up operations around the whole area and our own company was kept very busy. In addition to this, there were the all-important guard duties to be reckoned with. Two soldiers were on guard together and they always had to be on the alert, not only for their own sakes but also for the remainder of the company and vehicles. After all, this campaign had only just reached a conclusion and there was always the possibility that enemy agents were up to no good. The most was made of what was expected to be the last opportunity to go into the sea, which was very warm and receptive. The weather was perfect; the lads would always remember their sojourn at Letojanni!

All these many years later, when I still read of the Sicilian Campaign, the memories, both sad and happy, return to my thoughts and I am proud of the minuscule part I played in what took place when we chased the enemy from Sicily with his tail between his legs.

Chapter 15

Our Return to England

THE DAY we left Letojanni, we were told that our division, together with the 51st Highland Division, was going back to dear old England. The news was totally unexpected because we all felt certain that we were going to Italy to join up with the Eighth Army. We were told that all stores and vehicles were to be handed over to a battalion which was taking our place. Anticipation was hard to conceal and even our officers seemed to be very light-hearted. Another episode of my war was over. It was a great feeling to be told 'out of the blue' that we were going home soon; of course then we did not know the reason for our return.

The morning of 17 October 1943 found us travelling over the dusty tracks along which we had gone weeks ago, but this time there was no danger and the journey was unforgettable. The track went back and forth across the sides of the mountain, then through all those miles of seedless grapes and tomatoes. The view across the whole landscape was fantastic. Nature was being very creative and extravagant when all this beauty, which became Sicily, arose out of the Mediterranean. Arriving at the port of Augusta on the island's east coast, we boarded troopship HMT *Otranto* and sailed the next morning. After my memorable journey on the *Queen Mary*, I soon came to the conclusion that I would not remember the *Otranto* with the same affection, apart from the fact that it was the ship which returned us to England. We were very crowded and most uncomfortable and, to add to the misery, the sea was rough, yet strangely I was not seasick, for which I was grateful. Maybe my earlier journey on the *Queen Mary* had prepared me in some way.

We arrived at the port of Algiers on 25 October, where we stayed for two days and made the most of getting on deck if there was space. Then we were on our way again to North Africa and I remembered all the ships and planes and lives which had been lost in this part of the Mediterranean during the siege of Malta, amidst the actions which had taken place to supply the island and also preventing supplies from reaching the Afrika Korps.

Arriving at Gibraltar, we only remained for twelve hours. Sadly, we couldn't go ashore, but I didn't hear anybody complain. Their thoughts were on more important destinations, for at the back of all our minds was that we were going back to England. The sea was rough again, passing through Biscay, but we were all good sailors by then and the discomfort on board was bearable because we were on the last lap to Blighty.

We were told over the tannoy when we would dock, but not where. 'When' was during the early hours of 5 November 1943 – bonfire night coming up. What a laugh – we had seen enough fireworks to last a lifetime! Anyway, it was a pitch-dark night, and raining too, and for security reasons there was no brass band to welcome us home. We could not see any sign of England, not even the White Cliffs of Dover which I had so remembered when I returned from Dunkirk (that seemed a lifetime away). But there would not be any white cliffs because devastation was all around. This was wartime, bombed-out Liverpool in the blackout, and we could hardly believe our eyes at the battering it had received during the air raids. It was a sight that some of today's 'do-gooders' should have had to live through and they would then understand why we retaliated so fiercely against Germany.

Not even our families knew our division was back in England, and right then we were really homesick and very, very tired. But it was a fantastic feeling to have the ground of our own country under our feet, even if it was wet, cold and windy. Some of the older lads, who had been away for two-and-a-half years – many away from their wives – had no idea of the battering England had gone through and what the people had suffered and how they would relive the horrors of war for many years. But landing at Liverpool was not the end of the road for us. There were many sad moments to come which would put our morale and stamina to the supreme test. What trauma yet awaited us? Thankfully, then, none of us knew.

Somewhere ahead lay our destination. Perhaps for a change, and a miracle, we would be billeted in a town where we could see people and, better still, girls – English girls – but it was not to be. We ended up at a Nissen-hutted camp called Riddlesworth, which was three miles to the east of Thetford, in Norfolk. It was light by then, so we could see the camp with clarity and other than the Nissen huts, the first impression was that it did not look bad, but first impressions could be deceiving, as we had discovered from the past and we did not take things at face value. However, as billets go, it was acceptable and more so because we had no sooner settled in than we were told that we would again be going on leave very soon. The three days we were waiting to go on leave were mostly spent on sleeping, letter-writing or playing cards. Also, miracle of miracles for us, we actually had a NAAFI in camp where we could listen to another miracle, a wireless. We had never had such luxuries. We had been paid for the first time in four months and issued with ration cards and travel warrants. We felt like lords. We had a good dinner to see us on our way and we were off. Transport took us to the station.

I must have travelled seventeen thousand miles since I had left England. Now we had returned and left hundreds of good boys behind, buried in foreign soil. How sad. This was one time we would not mind sitting on our kit bags in the corridor of the train and we had done that many times. We could even sleep like that. Just sitting there, reminiscing about yesterday, thinking of now or tomorrow all gave way to somnolence. The trains were always crowded with uniformed personnel, so most of us slept anyway. There was no singsong because it wasn't as if the train was fully occupied by our own lads, but we didn't care so long as the train was travelling north, where most Green Howards lived.

Riddlesworth camp had been left with a skeleton staff to get the place organised for our return from leave, but our return was not on our minds now; all that mattered was indeed now. We had seen enough of what happened to our tomorrows; live for today.

During my entire time in the army, I was only granted fifty-six days leave, apart from the weekend passes I was able to get when I was within a reasonable distance from home. A funny thing always puzzles me, even now. Although it was always a great feeling to be going home for a spell, I cannot recall anything significant about my leaves except this leave, after my return from the Middle East. Before the war I was a member of the Methodist Church so whilst I was on leave I went to Church and prayed for the pals who had given their lives fighting for their country. I also thanked God for watching over me and bringing me home safely. Then there were several specific duties I had to perform which were extremely trying and sorrowful.

Firstly, I went to Stockton, which was only six miles from where I lived, to see John Bousfield's mother and two elder brothers who lived just a few miles from my hometown. I told them John had been killed at Wadi Akarit but did not say how he had died. I said that these things happened so suddenly in war that John had gone to heaven without suffering. I am afraid that they were so wrought with grief at the loss of their lad at only nineteen years of age that there was no consoling them. I therefore came away very upset.

Then to Arthur Oxley's home. I remember the remains of the shattered body it was my duty to bury at Akarit. Again, understandably, my visit to his mother turned to great sadness. Thank goodness there was no possibility of her knowing how her son had died.

I had a pre-war pal called Don Savage. He was only eighteen and a grand lad who had been camped at Crediton near Devon in 1939. We had been good friends. When he left the grammar school, he joined the RAF, becoming an air gunner on Lancasters. When he went on one of the bombing raids, he was posted missing, never to return. He was a splendid scholar at grammar school and when I visited his home his mother, naturally, was heartbroken.

Then I went to see the parents of my pre-war pal, Bill Collings, killed on HMS *York*. They could not possibly know how their son had been killed. What an epistle this is. Of course, as I mentioned earlier, Bill had a younger brother, Vernon, who had died from a fatal bug. Their parents were inconsolable; two lights in their lives had been extinguished. Well, I had done my duty, but it was a dreadful leave, the only one where I vividly remember what I did. Those pitiful memories I will never forget.

After my sad visits I went home and, as usual, I had no sooner put my foot across the step than everybody wanted to know what I had been up to during my time away, which was understandable. But for my own peace of mind I did not say anything about the gory details of death. I was soon on my way back to camp on the usual overcrowded trains, sitting in the corridor on my kit bag. There never seemed to be a seat on trains in those days and there was always a long wait at transfer stations.

I never had a problem about returning to my unit. I feel certain I missed the comradeship which is prevalent among soldiers, especially after having fought together. Seeing so much death and at the same time watching out for each other, going through the same harrowing experiences, gives a lad a tremendous feeling inside.

At Riddlesworth, most things had been organised and it was great to be able to go to the NAAFI when we were off duty, just to sit on a chair (we never had chairs in our billets) and have a cup of tea (one penny) and a cake. We also had a good metal bed and three wool blankets, which was heaven, as it was a site very exposed to the elements, with a bitter cold wind. Mind you, it was November and we had just returned from the hot climate of the Middle East. Come to think of it, comfort in the army in my day was a rare thing. Usually the only place we had to sit was our bed and then more often than not we didn't even have that as on very many occasions we slept on a straw palliasse on the floor. During my whole time in the army I never saw a bed sheet or even pyjamas, though they would have been a nuisance, anyway.

There was no serious training undertaken as they were giving the lads a good rest for what was to come, which was to be soon. Several trips were made to the firing range to keep our eyes up to standard and also to keep the lads occupied.

When we left Sicily, all stores were left behind and taken over by the replacement units. Now, during eleven weeks at Riddlesworth, our division was being totally re-equipped to a much higher degree than ever before.

All rifles, guns, trucks and Bren gun carriers had been brought in. It's strange in the army. One is either abroad fighting for one's life, never knowing the second one would be killed, or stationed in England being bored to death doing routine, everyday tasks. We had reveille at 0600 hrs, a wash and shave in cold water, then PT, make up beds, mess time-out and queue for breakfast, then maybe a long route march in full kit, taking turns carrying the Bren gun. Trouble was that there were no avenues of pleasure to relieve the boredom, just the same old tough routine.

We had no illusions about our return to England. Although the war was going well, it was far from over and there would be much for our division to do to help bring it to a successful conclusion. The invasion scare was well and truly now part of history and, therefore, the next episode in the struggle must be the invasion of Europe but at that time nobody knew anything about the role that our 50th Division

My first car was a Morris Ten and had been bought new for £187 – a lot of money then. When war broke out I was camping in Devon with pals and we had to belt back up North in this car. Southbank, Yorkshire, 1936, aged 19.

Taken at Alexandria, Egypt, in May 1943, Aged 26.

Major Petch, my company commander at Dunkirk. I was his batman for a while. He certainly cared for his boys.

Troops wade into the chilly sea at Dunkirk, queueing patiently to board a waiting rescue craft, May 1940.

The dreaded Stuka dive bombers which caused havoc amongst both troops on the Dunkirk beaches and innocent refugees fleeing from the danger zones in Normandy.

Just after Dunkirk with two of my pals after our grim experience, June 1940. I was 22 years old.

Mrs Margaret Jones, from Fairwater, Cardiff - one of the ladies who befriended me when I arrived at Cardiff from Dunkirk.

Tea and croquet, Highcliffe, July 1940. Jack Cargill (pictured) and I were invited here by these ladies after Dunkirk.

Alfred Decker, from Bremen, a prisoner of war I looked after at Qassasin Camp in Egypt. January 1943.

Alfred Decker wearing British battle dress at Fayid, Suez, 5 March 1941. This would be before his capture.

Dawn at Wadi Akarit – 6 April 1943. A Daimler Armoured Car fires 2-pound shells across the plain towards the enemy-occupied hills in support of the advancing allied troops .

Allied troops round up prisoners around Jebel Fatnassa, Wadi Akarit, in the late afternoon. Several allied battalions fought a hard but successful battle on this range and a number of my pals were killed here, including John Bousfield, Arthur Oxley and Lance Corporal Coughlan.

The day after the battle - a Sherman tank crosses the anti-tank ditch during the advance at Wadi Akarit, 7 April 1943.

John Bousfield from Stockton, Yorkshire - a good pal. Killed by an allied mortar bomb in the Wadi Akarit battle. Aged 19.

The shell-damaged cap badge of pal Arthur Oxley, of Durham, killed at Wadi Akarit. I only realised who I had buried when I found his dog tags afterwards.

Taken at Alexandria with my pal, Charlie Lee, of Selby, Yorkshire, May 1943. He was missing in action at Sicily but there is no trace of Charlie in public records.

With George Bertram, from Durham. Taken in Alex whilst on 3-day leave. I believe George survived the war but I never learnt what became of him.

He polished his 'soja's' boots every day of my stay in Alex - even when they didn't need it!

Jack Betley, 20, from Halifax, killed in Sicily by machine gun fire, 14 July 1943.

Alex Mill, one of my pals at Mareham-le-Fen. Killed in Sicily in 1943. There is no trace of Alex in public records.

Good old Bristow, from Surrey, was the nicest cockney I ever met. He was killed in Sicily in 1943. There is no trace of him in public records.

The 6th Battalion's Bren guns in action on the Catania Plain, Sicily, July 1943. (*Supplied by courtesy of The Trustees of the Green Howards Museum, Richmond, Yorkshire*)

General Montgomery stops his car to talk to Royal Engineers working on a road near Catania, Sicily, on 2 August 1943. A few weeks after this I would prepare hor's d'oeuvres for his meal with General Eisenhower.

Troops storm off the landing craft onto the beaches of Normandy, 6 June 1944.

Green Howards of 69 Brigade mopping up near Tracy-Bocage in the Normandy bridgehead on 4 August 1944. Notice the knocked-out half-track.

The sinister view along a woodland trail in Normandy.

A Hobart Flame Thrower ejects its deadly contents into an enemy stronghold, the Germans strategically holed up in a coppice.

The piece of shrapnel which wounded me in the thigh shortly after D-Day. It was part of an 88mm shell.

Lance Sergeant Allan 'Rufty' Hill, died tragically on D-Day during the landing on Gold Beach. He was a great scrapper. Previously unpublished photo kindly provided by his nephew, Mike Smith.

At Dundee Royal Infirmary, wearing my Eighth Army ribbon. I am leaning to one side because of the wound in my other leg. L to R, Top: Peck, Me, Allen, Hunter, Rogers, Underwood. Bottom: Broughton, Nurse Fowlis, Turner. Aug 1944.

Rufty Hill (back right) and friends with Bill Vickers (back left), his close pal. Taken at Limassol, Feb 1942. This heart-warming, previously unpublished, photograph was kindly supplied by Rufty's nephew, Mike Smith.

Brugge, March 1945, before we went to the front at Hamburg. Four of us are in the same tent. Army life was really nothing like this, which was only a very brief interlude. Tommy Chaffe at my side.

In my best uniform as a Regimental Policeman providing security at a German sports gala at Duisburg. All the civilians by that time had accepted their lot and showed no sign of resentment towards us. It was a lovely day in October 1945.

My pal Tommy Chaffe, one of the better Cockneys, in the East Lancs. Hamburg, Germany, October 1945. Tommy survived the war but I have never heard from him since.

Jack Spooner, my pal from Sheffield, was in the orderly room at Riddlesworth in 1943. He typed the words to Lily Marlene for me. He survived the war and had two sons.

With Harold Greenwood at Bold Venture Park, Darwen, Lancs in 1946. Harold was my best pal in the East Lancs.

With my wife Anne whom I met through Harold after the war. We were married in 1948 and this photo was taken on our honeymoon in the Lake District.

Paying my respects at the graves of fallen comrades at Bayeux cemetery, France, on the 50th Anniversary of D-Day, June 1994.

HM Queen Elizabeth, President Mitterrand of France and the Duke of Edinburgh sign the guest book at the memorial service at Bayeux.

The procession is about to start leading to the beach parade at Arromanches. It was an emotional experience for many of the veterans.

Beach parade at Arromanches. Note the Mulberry Harbour and DUKW's (amphibious vehicles) in the background.

Father and son in Bayeux cemetery car park at the end of an emotional holiday and a wonderful day on the 50th Anniversary of D–Day, 1994.

would play. Our division had seen a great deal of active service and was staffed, in the main, by very competent officers. We knew that we had been brought home so we could make a major contribution towards bringing the Germans to their knees.

At Riddlesworth, I was kept rather busy as I once more took up my job as company officers' cook. The guard would awaken me at 0500 hrs every morning and, after I had performed my ablutions, I would make my way to the officers' mess hut, which included a kitchen with a first-class range. Next to it was a dining room, which was next to a very comfortable officers' mess. I would make myself a cup of tea around 0520 hrs and prepare for the cooking of breakfast. Next came early-morning tea for the officers, which the batmen would collect to awaken their officer. After breakfast I would go to the main cookhouse and draw rations for the day; there was always an excess so nobody, including the lads, went short. After breakfast, the duty officer would see me to discuss the menu for the day, depending upon what rations had been issued. I never had a problem being able to converse with our officers. They were always willing to talk easily with the other ranks and I know all the ranks appreciated it. Having settled on the menu, I would tidy the kitchen because I was scrupulous and liked to be organized in many ways. I didn't have need for any assistance in the kitchen, since there were only five officers and yours truly. At about 1000 hrs my pal, Jack Spooner, from Sheffield, who was on the staff in the orderly room, would call in for a chat and a cup of tea with me. He once typed out the words to Lily Marlene for me. He was a good sort, Jack, and we were good mates.

An officer might sometimes pop his head in the door and ask: 'Any tea on the go, Cheall?' I always made fresh tea. I hated the brew which was permanently on the stove and where one just added more water and tea till the spoon stood up in it! Cocoa was always on the go at suppertime.

If only I could have looked ahead fifty years, I would have seen my wife and me moving home to live very happily in a village near Cambridge and only twenty miles from Riddlesworth, which I now pass very often.

The cosy set-up at Riddlesworth was not to last too long because during the third week of January 1944 we packed up once again. It was to be Southwold in Suffolk this time; right on the coast, and we were billeted in requisitioned private hotels on the edge of the small town. But almost all the time we were short of money and a visit to the pub for a drink was a real night out. Still, Southwold was fine.

At this time, we were lucky enough to have a show put on for us by Cyril Fletcher at the Pier Theatre. But we had no sooner settled in than we thought, 'They are mucking us about again', a remark often passed in those days. All the new stores and equipment we had received at Riddlesworth so recently were withdrawn and everything was replaced, but it was not our job to wonder why, just to do it. I was still cooking at Southwold and made my pal a wedding cake there.

Training was beginning in earnest as we received many new recruits here who had never seen active service and they had to be toughened up. But it was a different kind of training to what we had been used to in the Middle East. We used different methods of attack and deployment, using sections, platoons and companies. We had, in fact, to learn a new art of warfare almost from scratch. It seemed stupid to us at the time but eventually, in Normandy, we realised the purpose behind the apparent madness – it was the bocage – but more of that later.

It was a good billet, overlooking the green, at Southwold. I went back years later and showed my wife where I had done my cooking. Unfortunately, another move was on the cards and in four weeks we were on the way yet again to a new training ground.

Chapter 16

Intensive Training

IT WAS March 1944 and the time had come for a higher intensity of training to be fit and ready for any eventuality. We were to become even more skilled at beating the enemy at his own game. It was going to be tough, rough and concentrated and, apparently, we would wish we had never been born, so said the instructors. We wondered what it was that we were being taken to. We would soon find out.

We were on a troop train bound for – well, that was anybody's guess – all we knew was that we were heading north, so kit bag seats to ease our discomfort were not needed as no other members of the forces were with us so there was seating for us all. No wartime soldier will ever forget journeys such as those. There were the card games and the good wartime songs which, fifty-odd years later, are still sung with gusto. Enjoying every second, we were real pals. Those songs, many of which were sentimental, made us think of home. All that without the swill they all drink today. No rowdyism or punch-ups, just honest-to-goodness comradeship. It was great. Then we would all sleep the sleep of the just until the train jolted to a stop, waking us up. No, we hadn't arrived at wherever we were going but there, waiting for us on the platform, were the faithful ladies of the Salvation Army and Womens' Voluntary Service. 'Come on, lads, it's hot, sweet and strong!'

For security reasons, we were never told where our destination was, and of course this made sense. It wouldn't do for Tommy to write home saying that 50th Division were going to such-and-such a place. Somebody said that walls had ears, but it seemed a hell of a long way and since we were still travelling north it had to be Scotland. At the time we had never heard of Inverary, northwest of Glasgow. So this was Scotland, in early March. It wasn't just cold, it was bloody cold! Inverary was a small town of about four hundred and fifty people, on Loch Fyne. We were going to get to know all about the course here in a little while. Still, it was somewhere different, so very different, and desolate. I had never been to Scotland but I was going to get to know it and love it over the next eighteen months, but at the time there were other more demanding things to be done and not very pleasant at that.

The reason for the training we were about to undergo, apart from making us very fit, was not apparent to us then, but it became very obvious when, in June, we were enlightened about many things we had been curious about. During our stay at

Inveraray, the weather was dreadful and we had never experienced such bitter cold, pouring rain and snow, but the weather hadn't to interrupt our training. The place was rough and tough and any weaknesses in our condition soon surfaced and were cured. Now we knew why those Scots lads of the 51st Division were a hardy lot. We would say: 'God, who would live in Scotland?' But that was at the start of the course. Later, when we realised how weak we had been, and how perfectly fit we were at the end, well, Scotland wasn't so bad after all.

The camp had been very specially prepared so that the soldiers completing the course would be at the peak of their physical fitness. When we left there were no weaklings amongst us. This was to be a commando-training course and it was to prepare us for strenuous times ahead. We were billeted in Nissen huts once more but these, because of the climatic conditions, were very warm and comfortable. Each hut stood in its own clearing and all huts were nestled amongst tall pine trees. How the wind howled through them. Everywhere looked desolate, wind-blown and very wintry, without any amenities or comfort whatsoever. Roll on time; the course hadn't even started yet. There was not going to be any spare time for us. It was a slog from the beginning to its conclusion. What a life!

We were told to stop moaning; it was not going to be a rest cure but a kill or cure. And it cured us! There were no common colds and sick parades weren't allowed. If there was anything wrong, tough, just get on with it. That was discipline with a capital D.

We really got stuck into what had to be done, although the first day or two played havoc with muscles we didn't know we had. We were urged on continually by regular commandos, with all sorts of training. On the second day, we did a forced march in torrential rain, never allowed to stand still, running up and around mountain sides and crawling through swampy ground and ditches, half full with mud, until we were up to the eyes with filth.

We went across ropes suspended over the river, which was fast flowing, though only three feet deep. Two of the boys fell into the water but there was a net across to stop them drifting away. There were ropes tied on strong branches of the trees and we had to climb up hand over hand. Everything was most strenuous. We also had a go at storming a beach from a landing craft. I wonder why we thought we would be taking part in an invasion. It was no place for the faint hearted! As each day passed, we all became fitter and fitter and it felt great. We were very well fed with good wholesome food and, being kept on our toes, the end of the course soon came in sight and time seemed to have passed quickly.

On the last evening, drink was provided and we all made merry and sang our heads off. The two weeks of hell were behind us. It was a sight for sore eyes when we saw three-tonners, lined up to collect us and take us to, again, nobody knew where. We felt not a bit sorry for the battalion taking our place; poor devils didn't know what they were in for. While we were at Inverary, many of the boys who had been in the campaign in Africa went down with malaria, but I was one of the lucky ones.

I learned at the end of the war that 50th Division had been brought back to England to land in Europe on the third day, but quite suddenly our role was changed and we were to take part in the initial assault, many of us having the experience of active service. Monty said this was a tribute to the fighting qualities of our division, which had been proven in North Africa and Sicily. This was the reason for the specialised training we were undergoing from the time we arrived at Inverary until we went into our confined camps ready for D-Day, but at the time, for security reasons, we were not aware of the real reason. This also was the reason for us being re-equipped for the second time since our return to England, and also why we were to spend a great deal of time on amphibious operations from February to June 1944.

We drove through the pleasant little town, waving to the folk and passing right alongside Inverary Castle and it really was a picture. We passed it only too quickly, making our way to Stirling railway station, where our special train was waiting for us and the lights in the coaches looked welcoming. The mountains looked fantastic with their snowcaps on.

At that particular time, there were no regrets about leaving Scotland, but I did not realise at the time that I would be back in no time at all and came to love what I saw and experienced with great pleasure. The seeds of future friendship had been sown.

The lads were making imaginary bets about where we were going, but this time none of us really cared, knowing that it must be somewhere in southern England. Meantime, the train sped on its way, stopping only long enough to have a mug of tea to go with the cheese sandwiches we had been given when we left camp and to stop for a good hot stew which had been arranged ahead of us. There were always our 'friends', the Red Caps, waiting at every exit of the station to make sure nobody went AWOL (absent without leave) or, as the lads used to say, 'bugger off'. Back on the train and the doors all clanged shut; we would settle down to snooze, our minds a blank. It would have been good to have a dream of home, perhaps even a dream that the war had ended. The following lines are taken from my diary and which I wrote a week after it happened:

'We had a long train journey before us and as we passed through the countryside of southern England, our troop train went under a bridge. All of a sudden, there was such a terrible screeching and crashing of coaches. As the coach which was second behind mine, was going under the bridge a lorry crashed over the parapet and crashed between two coaches, across the couplings, and separated the train. The first coach just seemed to concertina and the following three carriages reared over it. They came off the rails and ploughed into the field on the left, turning onto their sides. It was a good thing the track was accessible from the road, about three hundred yards away, and it didn't take

long for the services to be on the scene. Injured and dead Green Howards lay all over the place.'

How could anything so tragic happen to us? Only minutes or even seconds before the lads were singing, joking or sleeping. How could God let it happen? They were mostly good lads who, because of our calling and profession and experiences, believed in the Almighty and although not ardent in their church going, prayed often. This tragedy should not have happened. How awful for the families of the lads who had been killed; many of them had faced death in North Africa and Sicily, surviving the bitterness of conflict, only to be plucked from the prime of their lives in England! The reality of it was beyond belief.

We had all seen sudden death many times, so our officers quickly organised us into sections to help the services with the clearing up operation. The greatest sadness was lifting the broken bodies onto the ambulances. Surely, this hadn't happened to the lads who had strained every sinew in their bodies during training in Scotland to be fit only to be killed in the twinkling of an eye in this way?

We had to hang around for some time whilst another train was brought up the line and, climbing aboard, we were all quiet, looking back at the tragic scene and somehow settling ourselves again. For quite a while, none of us spoke of any particular pal who had been taken from our midst. For professional reasons, we had to overcome the enormity of the accident, but for the remainder of the journey there was no singing or jokes or hilarity. We would remember today.

It was 13 March and Boscombe, Hampshire, was our next stop; the town was only about nine miles from Highcliffe where I was billeted in 1940. During our stay at Boscombe we lived in a very good hotel, called the Burlington, which had been requisitioned and was now always occupied by troops. It was a splendid, large building on the cliff top, about five hundred yards from the beach. We would fall in, in platoons, and run along the road, then down about forty steps and across a pedestrian bridge, then down a zig-zag path to the beach and do a two-hour stint of strenuous exercise and then we would run length-wise in two feet of sea. It was too bad if we fell over! Apart from the training on the beach, we did have a good rest here – it was all a laugh after Inverary. The stay was easy and we slept like logs on our palliasses – well, who needed luxury accommodation anyway? (We did!). The only real training was every third day, when we would be transported to bombed-out buildings at Southampton and made practice attacks on part-demolished property. We shouted and yelled at an imaginary enemy and, using live hand grenades, gained experience in street fighting. This was a thing we had never done before, even at Inverary. The experience was invaluable to us and probably more so to the NCOs and officers who had not been in action before, having joined us as replacements for casualties sustained in the Middle East.

It is strange how small things stick in one's mind. Just a hundred yards from our billet there was a small café run by the YMCA to which we had to climb ten steps. It was great, because we did have some spare time then and used to sit and chat over a cup of tea or beans on toast and other light meals, as well as cakes, and listen to the wireless. What luxury! Boscombe, apart from the pubs, was a typical seaside town in winter, although it was acceptable since it was the first time I had actually been stationed right in a town and the residents were very tolerant towards us. Well, we were all good lads, weren't we! But this short respite soon came to an end and once again, we were on the move, going to Swanage and Weymouth, finishing up in no time at all with a return visit to Studland Bay. Here, we learnt new techniques about landing on the coast from landing craft, carrying the utmost weight of equipment and weapons. In those days it was a desolate dump but at the end of the day we were there to do specialised invasion exercises, not to take a holiday.

After being taken out to sea a couple of miles, the assault craft would turn around and at speed make for the beach. We jumped into three feet of water after the ramp went down, then hastened up the beach to attack an imaginary enemy – just as in the Gulf of Akaba before Sicily. Of course, we were certain that we would be invading somewhere in the not-too-distant future. It was all very well assaulting a beach, but it is the live ammunition which makes the difference. I got the impression that it was the intention of a higher authority to make us as wet as possible, as often as possible, and then to send us on a cross-country manoeuvre whilst our clothes dried on us, but this did not even begin to give us an idea of what the real invasion would be like.

We did several long route marches and exercises around Corfe Castle and back without any halts. It all seemed rather elementary after the training in theory and actual battle conditions we had experienced, but it kept us at the peak of fitness, ready for the fray we felt could not be too far away, and for which there had been very little precedence for the massive operation facing us, yet strangely enough we seemed to have an insatiable appetite for action.

Studland Bay was only a short stay and the beginning of April saw us at yet another place…

Chapter 17

Time For Action

STUDLAND BAY had been rather bleak and, once again, we were pleased to be on the move, always on the move. I don't know how the Military kept in touch with where we were but my record has every detail of my movements. All credit is due to the records office.

The first week in April 1944 found us at a new campsite, in bell tents which had been erected in a field of short grass. It was Bushfield Camp, two miles outside of Winchester. We certainly got around in the army. I recall we were under canvas and luckily it was good weather. The battalion field kitchen was set up in the middle of the field and at meal times the bugle would blow and the lads would grab their mess tins and eating irons and join long queues in order to be served with their meal, which was usually plentiful. But I don't know why the army could not have provided waitress service for its infantry!

In the field adjoining ours, there were some American soldiers who appeared to be from a different planet. Their attitude seemed to be so easy-going and casual. No bell tents for them, but good square tents with three-feet walls holding about a dozen soldiers. We had six to a tent. The smell from their kitchens was fantastic; they even had doughnuts for afters. We had rice pudding most times. I didn't think they looked as fit as we were and they appeared to be casual in their movements. But they were very well equipped and I was sure that they would give a good account of themselves when the time for action came. They were our allies and it was hoped that we could learn from one another. They were very good-natured and always greeted us as friends. Being the first US soldiers we had come across, we were certain to get along well – they were OK.

We were taking it easy at Bushfield Camp as everything was so relaxed. It wasn't natural to have so much time to ourselves. They must have thought we needed a rest! We spent more time cleaning our weapons than ever before, which was not a bad idea since our lives could depend upon them. I think that right now, fifty years on, I would love to recapture some of the atmosphere of those days and get my hands around a Bren gun and Lee Enfield rifle, just to handle them and clean them.

I did foot slog into Winchester a couple of times but it wasn't my sort of place. A week after arriving at Bushfield we were on the move again, moving ever closer to the day we knew nothing about – yet – but felt that it could not be so far off. The new camp was a great contrast to Bushfield and we were not going to like it. Again, bell tents – always 1914-18 bell tents – which had been pitched among trees on stubbly grass and the ground was sandy, ideal for the colonies of ants which pestered us. It was the second week of May 1944 and we were three miles from Romsey, on the Winchester Road, which passed about twenty yards from our tent. It was drizzling with rain much of the time and weapon cleaning was a nightmare, not exactly a tonic to put us in high spirits. For a few days at first, only routine work was done and we made a few hikes into Ringwood. We did not know at the time that we would be at Romsey until the great day but things were becoming very intriguing. Around 23 May, outgoing mail was suddenly stopped and we were confined to camp. Yet I can recall that the camp was not guarded to keep us in; it was only a verbal order which was obeyed without any questions being asked. Anyway, who would want to go to the nearest pub and talk his head off and perhaps jeopardize the whole thing? In any case, all bus and railway stations would be watched by the Red Caps and they stood no nonsense; they would be on the look-out all over the south of England for any soldiers going AWOL. Significant events were taking place. During this period we had not been enlightened about any plans but we did not have to wait long. Our officers obviously knew more about the goings on than we did and they were not saying. It appears that our 50th Northumbrian Division and the 51st Highland Division had been brought home from Sicily to land on the continent after the first day. Then Monty changed plans for a wider frontal assault; 50th Division would now have to go in with the initial assault, details of which, later.

A large tent had been erected among the trees and each platoon, in turn, surrounded a sand table and looked eagerly on while a senior officer with a long cane demonstrated. The display was about the size of a table tennis table and covered with about two inches of sand with miniature tanks and buildings of all kinds. This was the first time we had seen a sand table and it showed every possible detail which we had to recognise when we landed. The way in which it had been set up was fantastic and we had looks of bewilderment and a genuine attitude of interest on our faces. The long side of the table represented the seaward side, showing models of all the obstacles the military knew we would have to face during the assault. Then, behind the beach, was a replica of everything we would find on the enemy coast. We all had our own sector to assault and on it, houses and all buildings, fences, tracks, hedges, streams and walls were depicted. We had to remember every detail as our lives could depend upon it and we should be able to see our position exactly in relation to other platoons and companies of the battalion. Naturally, we were not given any details about when or where in the world we would be landing; we were well aware of the need for paramount security.

The planning was on an incredible scale. Officers explained everything we needed to know about our area. Considering the variety of training and exercises we had been undergoing during the past few weeks, it was obvious that we would be playing a significant role in any invasion, whenever it came. All kinds of questions were encouraged except about where it was going to be. It was a miracle how everything was kept so secret. Our lives would certainly depend upon security.

We also received an hour-long pep talk from our commanding officer about what was expected of us and the general state of the war situation, the intention being to boost our morale. However, there was no cause for concern. Our spirits were never better. The Green Howards were a grand bunch of lads from the North Riding of Yorkshire and no square head was going to have it all his own way when we were finally confronted with him. We had to avenge Dunkirk and the enemy was going to find out what a fighter the British soldier was.

The newer lads would not be able to imagine what the rest of us had seen during those anxious days for our country but they were good lads, as we older and wiser lads well knew. It was unnecessary for us to motivate them. We knew where all our priorities lay. Upon reflection, the pre-invasion days were amazing. Many seeds of friendship were sown during that momentous period. It was to be a time which would go down in history and our division was to play a significant part in the making of that history. As we were undergoing all this enlightenment around the sand table, other things were taking place on the road just about fifteen or so yards away from us. Heavy vehicle noise made any further talks impossible, so we went to investigate.

Overhanging trees forming an archway covered the road, which ran a matter of fifteen yards from our tent, and there was a six-foot grass verge. As far as the eye could see, armoured vehicles, trucks and guns of all sizes were parking on the grass verge, nose-to-tail on both sides of the road. It was a most incredible sight and we had never seen anything like it. There were hundreds of fifteen-hundredweight trucks, three-tonners, twenty-five pounders, anti-tank guns and many other weapons of war.

But the most impressive sight was the tanks – tanks we never knew existed – and at that time we did not know what their role in war would be. We soon found out. They were to be known as 'Hobart's Armour', named after the warfare expert Percy Hobart, who invented them. Today, all these new ideas are common knowledge but in 1944 the lads couldn't stop talking about what we were seeing. It was something we would never see again. The armour continued to build up and there were tanks with flame throwers on the front of them; tanks with revolving chains (flails) on a drum on the front to beat the ground and explode mines; tanks which could lay a matting in front of them to go over soft sand and over soft banks. They looked so incongruous, having their exhausts high in the air and the engines waterproofed so they could travel through water. All these vehicles were to land on the first day and needed to be so equipped until we had a port. This must have been a monumental task.

While we were at Romsey, it was impossible to comprehend the meaning of whatever we saw and heard. How could we have imagined the momentous decisions which had taken place concerning what was necessary to be done, in order to free Europe, or what part our 50th Division had to play alongside other units taking part in the initial assault? There was much for us to be told about before we set foot on the beaches which the enemy seemed determined to deny us. But we would be going into the attack with a determined state of mind about the formidable task facing us. There was no doubt about our resilience. We knew that every eventuality had been provided for and felt confident that we could make a successful landing. What had been instilled into our thoughts was the fact that we must succeed. We were very perceptive about what had been done to aid us in every way.

On 31 May all kit, except what we would carry, had to be handed into the stores. I made sure my two-inch mortar was clean. That would be staying with me.

Chapter 18

D Minus 1 to D-Day

ALL OUR efforts and training over the last months, ever since we had returned from the Middle East in fact, only had one end in sight – the invasion of Nazi-dominated Europe. So very much depended upon what we, at the sharp end of the assault, put into practice after we had rehearsed for it. If the arrowhead was destroyed, the breaking of the shaft would follow and we would be thrown back into the sea.

It was the first day of a not-so-flaming June 1944; army transport arrived and we were taken to Southampton docks, the beginning of a never-to-be-forgotten experience. We were not sorry to leave the camp at Romsey. Although we felt fully confident about the task ahead of us, how could anybody say, for certain, that God would be watching over us when we took the first steps towards the liberation of millions of people, who had been under the cruel heel of the Nazis for four whole years?

I was sitting on the tailgate of a three-tonner making for the docks and looking back along the road. It was tremendously exhilarating; we were on our way. As we passed along, I had a bird's eye view of all the armour on both sides of the road. I saw the crews of all the vehicles parked on the grass verges; they were having a smoke and no doubt, whilst waiting their turn to move, were chatting about the huge task they were taking a vital part in. Everybody had a very important role to play in Act One. Each of those boys, some of them not yet nineteen, would be putting every effort into what he knew his particular part in the performance was. There would be no more rehearsals for the show. A great responsibility rested on the shoulders of those tank crews and the entrance was of the utmost priority.

In the spearhead there were young men from all over the British Isles. I knew that the brave Canadians wanted to avenge Dieppe and that the American boys needed to see that the war with Germany came to a conclusion so that they could settle their outstanding account with Japan over Pearl Harbour. They would give their all, every one of them, and whilst sharing such dangerous experiences, would create an enormous bond of comradeship.

I can't really explain the feeling I had when I saw just a fraction of the massive power that was going to back us up when we invaded; I felt proud to be British. I say 'British', because although I am a Yorkshireman, I came into contact with some tremendous characters among the Welsh, Irish and of course the Scots, who were very often fighting alongside. It was an education to meet such lads. The 50th and 51st divisions were almost always together.

It was about 1030 hrs as our vehicles sped through Romsey. Any civilians who were about turned and stared as we passed them. They waved and showed great enthusiasm, giving the victory sign. They would know that we were on our way because they had lived in the midst of the preparations and were intelligent enough to know what we were about to take part in. It seemed almost incomprehensible that within a short time we would be fighting for our lives, somewhere on the continent. We were on the threshold of a momentous occasion. The route to the docks was overseen by the Military Police and there would be no stopping for any reason on this trip, until we were inside the dock gates. Then, we were at the beginning of a never-to-be-forgotten experience – indeed, the making of history.

Things were going ahead so fast and there was an overflowing tide of memories being stored away in my brain. This was the beginning of a period in our young lives and country that would be talked and written about for generations to come. How could we possibly have known then that so many years ahead of that day, the peoples of Europe would show great reluctance to display gratitude for what many of our lads had given for their deliverance from tyranny?

The ship we boarded was an American-built vessel. It was a Liberty ship, so-called after the statue of the same name. It was a new concept in shipbuilding, welded together as opposed to the British method of riveting. It was possible, the American way, to produce much-needed transport at a greater speed. I wonder if any of these ships ever came apart under the battering of the sea because of the method of construction. However, Liberty ships filled the void, which had been caused by sinkings, and they carried millions of men across the Atlantic, to their destiny.

My ship was called *Empire Lance*. We were very crowded, but didn't expect to be aboard for very long. But when we were allocated sleeping quarters, we decided we could not be going just across the Channel; all that information was yet to be given us. We had tiered bunks and after we had stowed all our gear we sat around chatting, putting the war situation into perspective. The lads soon started to lose any apprehension they had and the usual topics of conversation cropped up – women, and what the French girls would be like. It was all quite natural and helped to relieve tension. Some of us wrote letters to be posted by the military at the appropriate time and we always had lads amongst us who had a gifted knack for telling jokes, usually smutty ones; it all helped us to form a closer bond of friendship.

As far as I can recall, our gear consisted of our 303 Lee Enfield rifle or, in my case, a two-inch mortar and six bombs. We all carried, in our equipment pouches, two filled Bren gun magazines (twenty-eight rounds in each) in case there was a hold up in the supply chain, three hand grenades, or 'Mills' Bombs', a bandoleer of fifty rounds of 303 ammunition, an entrenching tool, a filled water bottle, a gas cape and groundsheet, gas mask, a full small pack and our webbing equipment, plus bayonet and steel helmet. Section leaders carried a Sten gun. We never travelled far without our small pack on our back; it contained a change of clothes and personal things. If anybody had spare capacity, more ammunition was carried because nobody was certain how things would go once we had landed and we were moving into uncharted waters against a formidable enemy.

Food was plentiful on board, as much as we could eat, which was a good thing since we needed to keep up our stamina. All other comforts had gone by the board. For two days to 3 June, everybody was wondering when we were going to get cracking; it was becoming a bit boring. Sometimes, we would lie on our bunks thinking and some lad would start talking about what he would do when it was all over and wondering if his girl would be waiting for him. Sadly, some of these lads would never see their girls again if fate played a tragic part.

Then, after three days of almost claustrophobic conditions, the tannoy system came to life, telling us to pay utmost attention. Our commanding officer then proceeded to speak. You could have heard a pin drop; no longer were we going to be kept in the dark.

It was to be France. That moment made the deepest impression in my mind. Our battalion would be landing on a three-mile stretch of beach between Le Hamel and La Riviere, having the code name King on the coast of Normandy, on a sixty-mile front. At last we knew. The whole attack from the sea would run from west to east, with the Americans on 'Omaha' beach, on our immediate right, and 'Utah' on our far right. The British were on 'Gold' beach, the Canadians on 'Juno', and the British again on 'Sword'. Then we knew we would be the first and it all began to come together; what we had been training for.

The invasion was so vast and complex that it was beyond our capacity to absorb it all. The part we had to play was of primary importance to us at that moment. Because of the different times of high tide along the coast, the assault would have to go in at staggered times, with our battalion going in as the spearhead of 69th Brigade. We would have to go ashore at 0725 hrs on the morning of 5 June. At last, we knew our destiny. We were only given information concerning our own front from then on. The talk had put us all in the picture and we all knew how very important it was to go into the battle with the determination and grit which had been drilled into us for months.

I don't know how the two hundred or so newcomers to the battalion coped with the news, because this would be their initiation, their first confrontation with the enemy. At least at that stage they would not realise how devastating war could be; that was only gained by experience. Most of us had, of course, faced the enemy several times but gave no hint to the new lads about what could happen in the battle. We gave them every means of support and when the critical time came, found they were made of good stuff, had stout hearts and soon learned the vital lessons of conflict. Then, after we had reached a critical point in our thoughts, the tannoy again came to life to inform us that the invasion was postponed because of the weather conditions – it was very windy and drizzling with rain. It now had to be 6 June, but all other information we had been given was to remain.

The wait was almost intolerable because now we all had even more time to think. We were all deep in thought about the possible outcome of the battle, anyway – we did not need more thinking time.

There we were on our ship, just waiting and keyed up, passing time cleaning our weapons and studying aerial photographs of the coast. Never before in history had such a formidable action been undertaken. The operation was massive. Though we were certainly not afraid, we were naturally a little apprehensive.

On the afternoon of 5 June our officers walked amongst us, giving the lads confidence, but there was always the boy who didn't give a damn. They cleared the air a lot with their wisecracks and later on made Jerry sit up. They were the tough lads of nineteen, some of whom were awarded the Military Medal for their exploits.

Then another request, not an order as such, came over the tannoy. The Padre, Captain Lovegrove, wanted to say a few words to us. Padres were always very kind and understanding and would always have something to say about their beliefs. We were given a short sermon and I will tell you, everybody listened. It gave us food for thought. Then we said the Lord's Prayer. God would watch over us. After the Padre was finished, our battalion commander began to speak and gave us a message from Monty, saying what he was expecting of us, knowing he could rely on our ability to put up a good show.

21 ARMY GROUP
PERSONAL MESSAGE FROM THE C-IN-C
(To be read out to all Troops)

The time has come to deal the enemy a terrific blow in Western Europe. The blow will be struck by the combined sea, land, and air forces of the Allies – together constituting one great Allied team, under the supreme command of General Eisenhower .

On the eve of this great adventure I send my best wishes to every soldier in the Allied team. To us is given the honour of striking a blow for freedom which will live in history; and in the better days that lie ahead men will speak with pride of our doings. We have a great and righteous cause.

Let us pray that 'The Lord Mighty in Battle' will go forth with our armies, and that his special providence will aid us in the struggle.

I want every soldier to know that I have complete confidence in the successful outcome of the operations that we are about to begin. With stout hearts and with enthusiasm for the contest let us go forward to victory.

And, as we enter the battle, let us recall the words of a famous soldier spoken many years ago:

'He either fears his fate too much,
Or his deserts are small,
Who dare not put it to the touch,
To win or lose it all'

Good luck to each one of you. And good hunting on the mainland of Europe.

B L Montgomery
General C.-in-C.
21 Army group
5 June, 1944.

Another message said that our ship would weigh anchor at 1745 hrs on 5 June and would sail with the armada to the coast of France. With the number of ships around us, we could barely see the water at all. By this time, the ship's engines began to throb. That was it; the time had come for action. We were on our way to make history; there was to be no more waiting, no more exercises; this was it. This was the big battle, 6 June 1944, and we were going to give the enemy something to contemplate.

For the purpose of this assault, we had been given an extra brigade – three battalions – for our division and they were to take Arromanches, as the Mulberry Harbour was to be set up in this section on the right end of our divisional assault. Altogether, 160,000 men would take part in the first landing and the whole invasion was named Overlord.

Before long, the Germans would know that the Allies were not going to be a soft touch. There was much to be avenged and a large bill to be settled. We were determined. We had undergone the training, we had the weapons, and we had good leaders; such was inevitable. That is how we had to think anyway and we were going into action with a positive state of mind. We were prepared even more than the Germans were in the early years of the war. Hitler was going to be beaten; no longer would he think he had the God given right to be victorious. These thoughts were going through our heads as we sang, 'Will I Live to See another Day'. Sadly, many of us would not see another sunrise. But for those of us who survived, the memories would be everlasting. We were making history in those days. I wonder if the young lads of today appreciate the sacrifices that were made by us so that they could have their today and tomorrow. I doubt it very much.

It was getting dusk as we put to sea and we were all below decks. It would have been good to see England from the sea but perhaps it was just as well that we couldn't as it might have made us think of home and this was not the time to let our concentration wander to things sentimental. The drizzle was still falling when we left Southampton and it would continue to plague us until late afternoon on 6 June.

I believe that any soldier, no matter what control he has over his feelings, would feel a little thoughtful about the outcome of what we were about to undertake. Beneath the surface, I am certain that he is aware of the fact that he might be killed. If so, how would he die? But once the attack goes in, that strange, natural feeling changes to one of grim determination. Death does not enter into the mind of a soldier in action; his mind is on what he has been trained to do – kill, or be killed. Fear does not come into the equation as he is alongside thousands of boys just like him and will not let them down no matter what. When the confrontation is over, that is another matter; they feel free to talk and express their opinion about what has gone on. I also feel certain that they thanked God for watching over them, when the outcome could have been so different. I confess that I often prayed during the war.

Over the years, I saw some lads who, after being in battle, just gave vent to their feelings and wept and trembled, out of control. These boys were not discriminated against in any way because we were all aware that lads of a particular nature just could not help showing their feelings in the aftermath. They had endured a very traumatic experience and they were by no means cowardly, because they had fought it well and extreme tension had built up within them. They were always evacuated to the rear areas where they received the care and understanding of our Medical Officer. Don't anybody ever condemn the attitude taken towards those boys. Anybody who faces an enemy just waiting to kill you and who will blow you to pieces, knows what an experience it is. Others, just keep quiet. You do not understand.

Few of us slept on the night of 5 June. Our thoughts were completely monopolised by what was going on around us and the thought of what tomorrow might bring. Most of the boys were very quiet, keeping their thoughts to themselves as we were well aware that a good number of us would be killed and the suspense was awful. We were facing the unknown, tomorrow, and the estimate of casualties did not improve the way we were thinking. Fortunately they were widely exaggerated, but could so easily have come true and were still bad enough. Many lads wrote letters to be posted after the invasion had started. Many went to their hammocks early and turned their backs to others, to be with their thoughts – alone – thinking about the loved ones they had back home, saying a silent prayer that God would keep them safe.

I feel sure everyone else in the invasion force was in the same determined and aggressive state of mind as we were, going forward with the intent to resolve. The weather in the Channel was the worst for twenty years and, to our cost, we soon found out for ourselves.

The agony of waiting was now over and on the morning of D-Day, reveille was about 0330 hrs. Everybody was soon on the ball, wanting to get going. We had kept our clothes on all night and sleep had been out of the question, apart from the odd forty winks. We made sure all our kit was to hand, then made sure we had a good breakfast, not knowing when we would eat again that day. Nobody was cracking jokes, just each lad with his own private thoughts, to be shared only with the Almighty.

Once again, the tannoy came to life to order us aloft. It was becoming a bit claustrophobic in our quarters, anyway, and we needed the fresh, salty air. We were breathing the dawn of a new day into our lungs. This day would liberate the oppressed, because we were going to be triumphant.

Many of us had been on deck for a few hours already, watching the flashes coming from the French coast. The paratroops had been about their fighting for three hours, holding the left and the right sides of the proposed beachhead, and the bombers were engaging the coastal batteries, though not very effectively as the early morning was misty.

There was still a little waiting to do and standing against the rail of the ship, looking down at the forbidding sea, my thoughts wandered back to the day when I was called up. Oh so many things raced through my mind; all the lads of the 6th Green Howards in 1939; they would have been glad to be alongside us, but instead, many of them had given their lives during the conflict; others were in prisoner of war camps, waiting for the end. Also, I recalled many things I had done and seen. From the beginning until now it was like reading a book, but now it was for real. The memories would stay with me to be recalled time and again as long as I lived.

At 0500 hrs, the ship heaved to. It was just starting to become light and we could hear, but not see, what must have been a huge number of planes passing overhead. The message came across for everybody to be on deck at their attack platoon positions. We were now standing waiting for further orders, almost weighed down with equipment, ready for the fray.

Suddenly, 'Come on lads, let's go!' from our officer brought me back very quickly to why I was there; it was time.

We had dropped anchor seven miles from the coast and could see a red glow in the distance. So much of history was now to be enacted and it was impossible to dwell on one thing. The Air Force had begun to play their part, as had others we did not then know about, and the endless roar of bombers and fighters passing overhead was deafening, interspersed with the roar of the guns from the battleships; we had great difficulty hearing commands.

It seemed ages ago since our platoon commander had shouted, 'Let's go' but in fact was only a very few minutes. Then I found myself with my leg over the side, trying to get a footing onto the scrambling net. I had fastened the mortars and bombs onto my equipment and my Number Two on the mortar was alongside me. It was not easy climbing down those nets at the side of the ship; the practice we had done for this day was nothing like the real thing and endeavouring to get a foot onto the landing craft was beset with danger. The sea was very rough and there was a three-foot rise and fall of the craft against the side of the ship. It was a hair-raising experience but, luckily, nobody suffered any injuries though the operation could not be rushed. Somehow, we made it and pulled away from *Empire Lance* and then waited until all assault craft were in line abreast.

There were fourteen assault craft to land on Gold beach, with thirty men in each. I was on the port side, fifth from the front of our boat. How could I forget? The first thing we all did was to get out our sick bags from on top of the grenades, in the right pouch of our equipment. As soon as we were all settled on the bench seat, the order came, 'Craft away'. We were only seven miles from our objective. This, then, was what we had trained for.

The whole operation was fantastic; the sea seemed to be covered with ships of every description. The run in was to take two hours and during that time, as the coast came nearer, we could not believe what was going on around us. Our H-hour was 0725 hrs, with the Americans on our right and because of the differences in the tide they had started their invasion at 0630 hrs.

God help us, lads!

Chapter 19

Grim Determination – D-Day, 6 June 1944

LOOKING AROUND us, we could see other assault craft taking station at each side of us. The sea was very choppy but as the mist began to clear and the light was improving, the whole mighty operation became visible to us. And what a sight it was – something nobody had ever seen before. The mind could not absorb the enormity of it all. There were thousands of ships of all sizes and, standing out like huge sentinels, the mighty war ships (in fact, almost seven thousand in all).

The extent of what we were taking part in is difficult to describe in great detail. It was such a vast undertaking that nobody, not even the participants who were part of it, could describe the invasion adequately enough and as vividly as we saw it happen. It would never be seen again in our lifetime. So many ships in one place at one time. If the British people could have seen it they would have been very proud. The sky seemed to be full of planes – bombers, Hurricanes, Spitfires and others I did not recognise; hundreds of them going towards our target for the day.

With the continuous barrage of the battleships' huge guns and the drone of never-ending streams of aircraft, the noise was deafening. Nobody would ever be able to paint a really true picture of what our eyes were seeing, and what it was like to be actually there would never be believed. If it wasn't for the tragedy of it all, the scene was magnificent.

When a soldier is going into action, it is not a time to think of the past, or the future. The present is the thing that is uppermost in his thoughts; what is happening now; today, is all that matters and God willing there would be another time for his tomorrow. He has to give his full concentration to what he knows he has to do. The probability of death does not come into the equation. Get on with the job.

Soon after we left our ship, we were able to look around us and see what was going on, especially when the sea lifted us up on a swell. We were not yet seasick. The mighty battleships firing their broadsides towards the coast, and the sight of our planes overhead gave us a great deal of confidence and encouragement to go forward with a stout heart. How could the enemy in their wildest dreams have imagined what the Allies would be able to assemble for this day, the day of retribution for the vile sins which had been perpetrated in the name of the Third Reich? What we lads were seeing would never be seen again and the folk at home would be proud of their men folk.

The infantryman was the vital link in the chain and we were the most vulnerable. We must not fall at the first hurdle but had to get ashore and move inland. If we did not succeed, the consequences would be very serious, so we would have to be aggressive. This memorable day in our lives will go into the history books and we shall be proud of it.

We were now seasick, that most awful of feelings, and were making full use of our sick bags but even that did not stop us from taking note of what was going on. Nobody wanted to miss this great occasion. Shells started coming towards us but the enemy seemed to be going for the ships, not us, and they created great spouts of water when they hit the sea. The gunners had not found their range. Now we could see bombs falling from our planes and fighters, skimming low above the enemy defenders. The continuous thundering was never ending.

We were about two miles from the coastline, Rommel's Atlantic Wall, when on our port side we saw something which we had never seen before. It was a rocket ship, about half-a-mile away from us, and it was firing a massive, continuous barrage of missiles, screeching simultaneously dead straight towards the coast. We could hear – almost feel – the heat generated by the displaced air. 'Hell', we said. 'Fancy being on the end of that lot!' It was fantastic and the bombardment was something the enemy could not have imagined it was possible to be on the receiving end of.

We could hear the rumble of war as the planes dropped their bombs. Warships were shelling the fortifications and the sound of the shells flying above us was uncanny. Great flashes were coming from the gun barrels and lit the morning sky. The battleships were firing their salvoes of shells, which we could hear screaming above our heads. And above them, the planes, a never-ending stream of planes of all sorts was going to bomb the communications inland so the Germans could not send for reinforcements.

Meanwhile, we saw the other assault craft keeping in line with us, in the hands of competent helmsmen, all rising and falling with the mood of the sea, like bucking broncos. As we were now coming within firing range, the enemy machine gunners turned their attention to us in the assault craft, and we felt fairly vulnerable, and not far from us we could see flail tanks which looked so incongruous, actually floating and moving just ahead of us, the intention being that they would clear the beach of mines; that was their primary involvement – mine clearing.

Whereas earlier we could only see and hear the guns of the warships, we were now between ship and shore and could hear the continuous scream of their shells above us. That alone was quite a sensation. They were certainly giving somewhere inland a pasting. This impression of what was happening around us was so fleeting and we had to concentrate on our own immediate situation.

It seemed to be a hell of a long way to the beach, then I saw a landing craft next to ours slow down. A bullet must have hit the helmsman. Swiftly, somebody took over control but the boat was now a little out of line with the other assault craft and in the blinking of an eye, the front of the boat had been hit by a shell or a mortar, or probably a mine. The explosion lifted bodies and parts of bodies into the air and the stern of the craft just ploughed into the sea. All those boys, laden with kit as they were, didn't stand a chance of survival.

The enemy fire made us keep our heads down and all we could do was watch the umbrella of planes above us. The noise was terrific; there is nothing I can compare it with, to try and convey to you the enormity of it all. There was so much happening now and so swiftly. Every second was vital; let's get out of this coffin! We were getting so near now and felt so helpless, just waiting for our fate one way or another and at that time we were keeping our heads down.

Enemy shells were now landing on the shoreline and machine gun bullets were raking the sand. Then, at the top of his voice, the helmsman shouted: 'Hundred to go, seventy-five to go, all ready, fifty to go!' He was now fighting hard to control the craft, avoiding mined obstacles showing above the water, as well as the ones just beneath the surface. One boat had already met disaster on the approach. 'Twenty-five yards', and suddenly, 'Ramp going down – now!' And the craft stopped almost dead in three feet of water and our own platoon commander shouted, 'Come on, lads,' and we got cracking. That was no place to be messing about. Get the hell out of it. Jumping off the ramp we went into waist-deep water, struggling to keep our feet. We waded through the water looking for mined obstacles, holding rifles above our heads. I was trying to keep a very cumbersome two-inch mortar and bombs dry as well as making certain I didn't drop it, as I was now carrying it as opposed to it being fastened to my equipment. It was impossible for me to keep the mortar dry but the six bombs would be OK in their sealed container. Some of the lads were shot as they jumped. Two of the lads were a bit unfortunate because as they jumped into the boiling water the craft surged forward on a wave and they fell into the sea. I dare say they would fight like hell and recover but we were not hanging about, that had been our instructions from the start; we must not linger.

Our adrenaline was now at its peak and every one of us was aware of what he had to do. At the moment there was no actual fighting to be done as there was no visible enemy, but we had to get off the beach and forward in order to come into contact because they were hidden in their positions. Our primary concern was to get out of the sea.

Onto the soft sand and the boys in front and behind of me went down. Hell, get moving! Halfway up the beach, about ten yards from the sand dunes, I saw an amphibious Sherman flail tank at a standstill, its chains hanging helpless like some monster, one track was off its sprockets. It had gone into the assault on the beach before us to make a path through the minefield which ran along behind the beaches. The crew had bailed out and had continued, under fire, to make a path across the minefield and had taped it.

Our old company commander from pre-invasion days, Captain Hull, (having been promoted to major) was on a signal ship and keeping in touch with proceedings.

On the beach, lads were falling all over the place. Resting with his back against the tank was our new company commander, Captain Linn, who had been wounded. He was waving his arm for us to get off the beach. Tragically, while he was in that position, he was hit again and killed. He was such a good gentle man, an excellent commanding officer and only twenty-seven years of age. Life can be very short in battle. I later visited his grave in Bayeux cemetery. Our platoon commander, Captain Chambers, now took over and he, too, was wounded but was able to carry on his duties. He was shouting and waving his arms: 'Get off the beach – off the beach, off the bloody beach. Get forward lads and give the buggers hell!' That was the natural leadership coming to the surface, though we did not need any urging because we knew that enemy machine guns and mortars would have previously been set up on fixed lines to cover the beach and were now playing havoc with us. It was difficult to make too much haste in the soft sand but, by a supreme effort, we ran up the slope towards the sand banks in face of heavy enemy fire.

Dead and wounded lads lay all over the beach, the worst of whom were shouting for the stretcher bearers, who were always close at hand to take care of them. They were bricks, those medics. At this time, we lost Sergeant Burns but I never did get to know how many others were actually killed on the day. Along the invasion front, 10,000 men were killed or injured.

From jumping out of the craft to getting onto the beach seemed to take ages, yet it couldn't have been more than twenty minutes, which was long enough to be in that situation and it was still drizzling with rain. I'll tell you what, we didn't look back. The situation didn't allow it, but now I wish I'd had the presence of mind to turn around to see the navy in action. It must have been an awesome sight from a defender's view, but this was no time for sightseeing. I had made it. It was beginning. Nobody, absolutely nobody, can even simply imagine the horror of war unless he actually experiences it. Take my word for it, it is awful seeing living boys killed before your eyes, heads and arms blown off. I could go on. Our company had suffered fairly heavy casualties; one platoon alone had lost twelve men, killed.

The way some of our lads died that day was dreadful. One of our sergeants, in D Company, was called Rufty Hill and as he jumped off the ramp into the sea he landed in a shell hole. At the same time a wave made the assault craft surge forward and he was forced beneath the boat. Rufty was drowned and probably crushed beneath the boat. I knew that chap and knew he would have given a very good account of himself had he lived to go into the assault. He was rough at the edges but he was a great scrapper and a good, tough soldier. It was a very sad loss to us all as he had always been a young man so full of energy, well known in the battalion and very popular with everybody. Nothing was too much trouble for him. He was 'one of the lads'. It was awful to think that Rufty had survived Dunkirk and from Alamein to Enfidaville then through Sicily, only to be killed in such a tragic way. For us, war was a very bitter experience in life. One can put these things to the back of one's mind, but how can one possibly forget? It is true when we say, 'They shall never grow old'. We will always remember them as we knew them, young and vibrant, good lads.

I was told that two lads who jumped into the water after me had been hit by gunfire, so I was lucky. Unless a soldier who was killed was one's pal, it did not seem to bother us as it happened so frequently and we did not dwell on the loss. A pal's death and how he died was a totally different matter and we were all aware how easily a good young life could be ended so violently.

Keeping as low as possible was the right thing to do but in the process, we were soaked to the skin from head to foot, but who cared so long as we got away safely? It was quite a heavy drizzle now and it continued until about 1600 hrs. Fortunately, with our exertions, our clothes soon dried out. Anyway, we had more important things to think about so our personal comfort was of little consequence.

The beach was the worst place to be. Since there was no protection, we felt very exposed and vulnerable and although still in great danger, felt better when we had entered the marshy ground beyond the beach. After all our haste and determination and taking about fifty prisoners and killing many of the enemy, to our great surprise, apart from the machine gun and mortar fire, there was not a great deal of opposition to our advance slowly inland. The outer crust had been broken, though there was some machine gun fire and always the snipers, looking to kill our officers.

After the initial landing had been accomplished, there was a different atmosphere among the lads and they could find time to light up their cigarettes for which they were all gasping. We now knew that we had overcome the unpredictable landing and what we now had to face were the usual hazards of war we all knew about. Our future would depend upon the discipline and self-confidence we showed in whatever action which faced us. All we lads of England would do what we had been trained to do. The beach, with all the deaths, was behind us. What had happened there was history, we just got used to it. The cold hand of fate did not lay its icy fingers on me, for which I thanked God.

D Company, on our right, was being held up by machine gun fire coming from a pill box and the sergeant major, Stan Hollis, who had always been an aggressive character when it came to killing the enemy, rushed zig-zag over open ground, firing his Sten gun and throwing a hand grenade through the door, killing the gunners and taking prisoners – several Germans in a trench – so saving the lives of many of his company. Stan, ever since Dunkirk, where he had been a despatch rider, had never shown a vulnerability to death. He always wanted to get to close quarters with the enemy and after the capture of the pillbox he performed other daring deeds, always showing great courage and determination. He seemed to have a charmed life. His performance resulted in him being awarded the Victoria Cross, the only one being won on D-Day. It was very fitting that he received his country's highest honour. In fact, he performed many daring deeds throughout his war service. For five years, from 1939 to 1944, he had risked his life many times for his country, his comrades and his regiment, The Green Howards.

After the war was over, Stan opened a pub in Middlesbrough; he gave it a very appropriate name, 'The Green Howard'. Unfortunately, Stan did not live to be an old ex-soldier able to sit and reminisce over the past. All his yesterdays went with him when he died in 1970. He will always be remembered by Green Howards all over the world and those of us who knew him personally will live with the memory of having served with him.

We now moved forward with great caution, expecting to come under enemy fire, keeping close to hedgerows in single file and our rifles at the ready. We could never become complacent, always on the alert, just as the enemy snipers would be. Up to now we had not seen an enemy tank. The countryside in Normandy was so different to any we had encountered in all our confrontations with the enemy, or even during all the training we had done in preparation for the invasion. It consisted of small fields surrounded by V-shaped ditches. The earth from the ditches formed a bank and, on top of the banks, hedgerows had been planted. It was called the bocage and, together with numerous small woods, was perfect country for defensive positions to be set up for snipers and machine gun nests, but very disadvantageous to attackers. So we had to be extra careful how we moved forward since we were in the act of forming the nucleus of a bridgehead on our sector and were hoping the other divisions had also been successful on their fronts so that a continuous line would be formed in case of any possible counter attacks. This is what we had to contend with mainly on that first day.

It was not just a matter of walking along country lanes because there was no shortage of enemy activity. One of our main objectives, about noon, was a rocket site, which was hidden in a wood about three miles inland. Heavy, intensive machine gun fire was directed towards us from here and, as the wood was isolated, we couldn't get near it. They seemed to be making a real effort to harass us and, in order to avoid any loss of life, our CO called up support. It came in the form of a Churchill tank. At a later date, when the RAF had airfields in Normandy, a Typhoon would quickly have been on the scene. Anyway, the tank advanced towards the wood and soon came under anti-tank fire and since it was not hit it retaliated, as quick as a flash. It stopped about forty yards from me and before you could bat your eyes – whoosh – it threw a huge tongue of flame towards the wood, doing so three times. Flaming Germans came running out from all sides with their hands up. The ones who survived were taken prisoner. Needless to say, the opposition ceased, enabling us to now move forward. Up to that moment we had never seen a flame-throwing tank in action. It was fantastic. For the remainder of full daylight hours we continued to advance, but as soon as the light deteriorated we had to be more vigilant than ever. We had a little way to go to reach the point which had been set for us and the enemy 88mm guns were still very active.

For the whole of D-Day we had not seen an enemy plane or tank, which greatly surprised us, though no adverse comments were made. On the other hand, our own planes had made every effort to keep overhead and it gave us cause for great confidence. Obviously, we had suffered casualties, which we regretted, but it had been a good day for taking prisoners.

All activity regards infantry ceased as soon as it was almost dark, though the long-range weapons continued to bother us. It had stopped drizzling with rain and we came to rest in a corner of one of the fields in line with the other companies. It was then that we laagered for the night, at least during the darkest hours, and defensive positions were taken up in platoon strength and leaving only sentries to guard us. Our resting place was on the edge of a field. After everything was to the satisfaction of our platoon commander he walked among us saying that we had reached seven miles inland and also expressing regret about Captain Linn and the other boys who had met their deaths during the day. He knew us all by name and was singing praises to us all, how well we had done and all the usual things. Most platoon officers were first-class and well liked by the lads, even cracking jokes with us. The cost in lives of our seven miles' penetration had not been excessive, regretful as the deaths were. He said we had done well, especially since nobody knew what faced us at the start of the day; the day the world, and particularly the oppressed peoples of Europe, had waited so long for.

After our officer left us we just sat around in twos and threes, talking, almost whispering, about any of our special pals who had been killed, but did not dwell on the subject of death very long. We dug down into our small packs for something to eat (apart from chocolate and Horlicks tablets we had not eaten since 0400 hrs, eighteen hours ago, a period of time during which a great deal had happened in our young lives). Yes, and dare I say it, a great deal of torment yet to come. We would have to wait and see. Tomorrow was another day and the enemy, knowing where we were, would not give up so easily. What we had for our meal was a can of ready meal. It was marvellous to us in those days. Just pull a ring, wait a short while and the can heated itself. We had never seen anything like it before, not even during the rehearsals for this day.

The drizzle had stopped during the afternoon and although we had been very wet we had now dried out and the activity of the day demanded that we try to get some sleep. Whether our restless thoughts would let us, we would have to see, apart from which, the odd shell kept coming across. Taking our ground sheet from our pack, we spread it out then, using our pack as a pillow, covered ourselves with the gas cape – no chance of a blanket. Since we had had very little sleep for three nights we should really have slept, but it still wouldn't come. The day's events, the horrors, the sadness, the things we had seen, kept us awake until we were called to go on guard.

That was how I saw D-Day, and I had survived to fight another day.

I opened my eyes as I lay on my back, looking skyward. There was still heavy cloud so the stars could not be seen. I then closed my eyes and thanked God for watching over me, then prayed to Jesus:

'The day thou gavest Lord is ended, the darkness falls at thy behest, to thee our morning hymn ascended, thy praise shall sanctify our rest.' This is, of course, the first verse of hymn number 667 in the Methodist hymnbook.

I then said to myself: 'Oh Lord, grant that the souls of our fallen comrades, who have given all in battle, rest in peace with thee in heaven, watch over us in the days to come.' I ended by saying the Lord's Prayer.

I felt I had done my duty, so I felt better and drifted into a restless sleep.

Chapter 20

D plus 1 to D plus 30

AFTER A few hours of restless sleep, we were fully aroused by the night guard touching our feet and very quickly we were alert. It was dawn; the most dangerous time not to have our wits about us. The gunfire had not yet rent the air, but it would not be very long.

There would not be any bacon, eggs and sausage this morning because it would take time and security for the field kitchens to be set up. There would not be any washing or showering either. That would have to wait. And shaving (it was only fluff anyway) was out of the question at the present time, while the invasion was at such a critical stage. Get up and go was the order of the day. During the twenty-four days I was in Normandy, the opportunity to wash hair or take a shower never arose. Other more important things occupied our time. We always had spare socks in our small pack, though.

There was soon frenzied activity. It was emergency rations for breakfast, as we well knew, so there wasn't any moaning. We ate chocolate, sweets, biscuits and a small box of raisins and of course there was a packet of Woodbine cigarettes and matches and since I did not smoke, I shared them out among my pals. Those were more important to some of the lads. Although many of them were only eighteen or nineteen years of age, almost everybody smoked. We knew that a good meal would be coming as soon as the situation improved.

Our battalion commander, having attended Orders group at Brigade, passed on relevant information to the platoon officers, who then passed onto the lads whatever details concerned our activities and hopes for the day – enemy allowing. It was good because we felt we were more than just a number in the infantry. Very often, when the enemy showed signs of resenting our presence, plans had to be altered and we would understand the problems that sometimes caused.

On D-Day, by early evening, other elements of 50th Division, on our far right, had liberated Arromanches, which was the proposed site of the prefabricated Mulberry harbour. It was the first place to be liberated during the first day of the invasion.

We now had our orders about the line of advance, who was to lead off, and other details. So on the early morning of 7 June, the company advanced, walking section after section, alternately, along either side of the narrow lanes, after a 'Good luck, lads' from our officer. On such occasions we always kept about three yards apart in case enemy shells landed near us, so there would be the minimum of casualties. In that respect the bocage helped us. The hedgerows saved us many times from the effect of shelling. On the other hand, the hedges provided cover for snipers and anti-tank gun crews – not that there were so many tanks at that early stage, unless they were operating in other areas. I saw very few on the first and second day.

We kept to the country roads, often for concealment, but there were also times when it was essential to move across open countryside. On one particular day, we were crossing a field on an incline when we heard planes coming towards us. Looking skywards, we could see the white stripes, which were the Allied marking for all aircraft during the invasion. They were our planes all right, fighters, but not very friendly. In a matter of seconds, they started to strafe us and we dived for the ground and made some attempt at becoming ostriches, but they had killed two of our lads. When the planes had gone, what we said I dare not write. The RAF was not a popular topic of conversation at that moment. Obviously, they must have mistaken us for enemy, but that was no consolation to us. Our officer, being a genuine sort of chap, said he thought that possibly there were enemy soldiers in the vicinity, so we deployed, crawling along muddy ditches in order to avoid being seen. We eventually surprised a patrol of five Germans who received the shock of their lives. They were not the arrogant type of German and quickly surrendered.

In past years, wherever we had fought the enemy, we had never had the proliferation of air cover that we had in 1944, especially as soon as our aircraft were able to use the airfields in Normandy. Now there were many new ideas coming to light relating to warfare and we saw many of these being put to very good use. After the third day or so, whenever we came upon a well-sited pillbox putting up stubborn opposition that could cause us casualties (which we had to avoid whenever possible) a message was sent to the rear and one or two Typhoons would appear in no time. On this particular day, the enemy were ensconced in a farmhouse and were putting up serious defensive fire and it was in a situation where we could not deploy around it without loss of life. Tanks would not approach too closely either, for danger of being fired upon by a hidden 88mm. Our CO, who sent a message to the rear, resolved the situation and our eyes were soon opened to the concept of combined operations. We heard planes coming towards us within fifteen minutes. There were two Typhoons, coming in low across the hedges and fields and whoosh – like flashes of lightning – two rockets went straight as an arrow towards the farmhouse and left a pile of smoking rubble where the farmhouse had been.

If only our young pilots of 1940 had had such weapons at their disposal. I should think that form of attack was also new to the Germans, who had had their days of glory when they had mastery of the air. How things had developed since the days of domination of the skies by the Stuka dive-bomber.

The above situation happened a countless number of times whenever we came across enemy strong points such as farms and church towers. In fact, any kind of suspicious building was quickly despatched by the Typhoons. They were brilliant. I once saw a Tiger tank suffer the same fate and there were no survivors, I can tell you.

Our advance was not always without its problems. Frequently, the enemy would be determined to hold us up. Then we would have to dig in, but the ground in Normandy being agricultural allowed us to entrench fairly quickly – just the opposite to North Africa, where much of what looked like deep sand soon became rock!

One day I came upon two dead Germans lying on their backs, open eyes staring at the sky. I searched the bodies, mainly on the chance of coming across a Luger revolver, which would have been a prized souvenir, but I was out of luck. What I did find was a photograph of the two of them and I still have it. I felt certain that somebody had been there before me, because their pockets were empty. It was the first time I had done that sort of thing, but some lads regularly searched dead bodies.

The advance was now only proceeding slowly because some units – and ours was one of them – were going too far ahead of the desired line. So to keep the front correct we had to fall back a little in case the enemy decided to counter-attack with a pincer movement and cut the leading units off. On this particular day, at about 1600 hrs, we halted and dug in, making our trenches about thirty inches deep to hold two lads sitting face to face.

Soon after we had finished, we heard planes coming in our direction and could tell by the peculiar engine noise that they were Jerries. It was a turn-up for the book because up until that time we had not seen a German plane since we had landed. Then they appeared, the black crosses and swastika so clear to us. Like a flash, they turned towards our lines, starting their dive, just as they did at Dunkirk when they had caused such chaos by their domination of the skies. It was an extraordinary experience, once again, to see the bombs actually leave the plane and to be machine-gunned us as the Stukas dived. They killed three of our lads. But the planes had no sooner pulled out their dive than two Spitfires came tearing across the sky. The Stukas tried to avoid contact, but did not stand a chance against the Spitfires. It was as if our planes were playing cat and mouse with them, but eventually we saw the Stukas break up in the sky then crash in flames.

Although our confidence about the outcome was already at a peak, it was good to see our planes in such a decisive action, and during my remaining time in Normandy I never saw another German plane. They had had their day and would never again strafe pitiful and helpless civilians. What planes they had left didn't stand a chance, as the retaliation was so swift and conclusive. This day, 7 June, one of our brigades freed Bayeux, the first town to be freed during the invasion.

The company settled down after the excitement and trauma of the day and it was my turn to do guard with another lad – two hours on and two hours off, which was different to the usual two hours on and four hours off. In a situation such as we were in, it was always essential to be constantly on the alert. Being on duty in pitch dark, when every move is magnified out of all proportion and a knife in the back is a distinct possibility, keeps a lad on his toes, every nerve straining for the sound of an enemy patrol. They too, would be silent, listening for the slightest giveaway sound!

Come the morning of the third day and surprise, surprise, the company cooks had been busy at B Echelon, just to the rear of us, and had brought up a hot breakfast. The verdict was unanimous. It was great. Mind you, we were a bit hungry and it was a sight for sore eyes. Once the field kitchens were operating, food was plentiful. Almost everything, so early in the campaign, was prepared from cans. Sausages, bacon, tomatoes, cheese, dried egg, milk, butter ..... . There seemed to be no end to what could be packed into a can. Such canned food was unheard of in those days and never before had we seen canned bacon. It was out of this world to us, delicious, and as much as we wanted with an ample supply of good, fresh, white bread. I'll bet the Germans could have done with some of that instead of their black bread. I seem to recall that only the precious tea and sugar were a loose commodity. But to us lads, what was as important as the food was the fact that some brilliant chaps had thought what a morale-boosting exercise it would be for the lads at the sharp end to receive mail from loved ones. Really, the whole effort had been well organized.

Needless to say, the cooks went to the top of the class and in our present frame of mind were promoted, immediately, to full sergeants. We did have our lighter moments, even under the strain of war.

So began another day. The expectation of enemy shelling was always present and we had not gone far when that expectation became realisation and orders came for us to dig in, just in case the shelling, which was heavier than usual, was the forerunner to a counter-attack. But after less than half-an-hour – in fact we had only just finished our trenches – the fire ceased. Just as well for the Jerries because the shelling had killed some of our boys and our adrenaline was at its maximum. They would have paid very dearly for the lives they had taken. It did appear, though, that the enemy were showing signs of recovery from the shock of the assault upon the Atlantic Wall and we were held in our position for four days. No explanation was given or expected. The enemy never did what we thought they would do, so we just waited and listened to the shells flying back and forth overhead. The mortars were always a problem and we suffered a number of casualties. The stalemate was eventually resolved in our favour and we pushed forward once again, always with the utmost caution, taking many German prisoners.

On 11 June, C Company was moving forward in our usual extended line across fields and, upon reaching a cornfield, continued to walk through the corn which was waist high, until we were half across. Then all hell let loose upon us from trees a hundred yards ahead, among which were snipers and machine gun posts. The snipers were after the NCOs and officers and they were very successful, too. It happened so suddenly and the first officer to be killed, by a shot in the head, was our company commander, Captain Chambers, who had taken over charge of C Company on the beach when Captain Linn was killed. We also lost a Norwegian officer attached to us – we all called him Norgy – a first-class officer and a gentleman. Several NCOs and other ranks were also the victims of the attack, including Major Honeyman and Corporal Alexander, Major Young, Bert Hall and a score of others were wounded. Our Company Sergeant Major was shot through the throat. It was quite a nightmare while it lasted. The angels must have been looking after me that day.

The remainder of the company dropped down into the corn and crawled out to escape. We were the lucky ones. We could all so easily have been killed. It was a severe warning to us not to drop our guard for a minute, because Jerry was still a crafty devil and would make us pay dearly for any laxity. It was also a warning to steer clear of cornfields. I can't imagine why we had to go across a cornfield at all, when all the enemy had to do was lob over a few mortars. It would have been catastrophic to us had the corn set alight.

Minor counter attacks developed and the odd German plane came over and of course the 88mm guns of the enemy were always a danger to us. On our right, German tanks broke through the positions of 8th Armoured Brigade and caused a dangerous situation, so much so, that we had to withdraw to straighten the line. We counter-attacked and the fighting was severe and determined, and lasted all day. One platoon of A company was surrounded for a while. All in all, it was a bad day for us, with a high proportion of officers and NCOs being killed – altogether 250 were killed or wounded. Our B company took twenty prisoners – all arrogant young Nazis. That happened on 12 June and we then dug in and consolidated our positions, after which time we were relieved in the line for 36 hours by a battalion of the 49th Division, and although we were able to get some sleep in, we were still harassed by the enemy shelling and mortars.

Because of the serious casualties, particularly in officers and NCOs, the battalion commanding officer, Lieutenant Colonel Hastings, had to reorganise the company when, once again, we were spread out rather more thinly until reinforcements could arrive. It took some days to put the cornfield fiasco to the back of our minds.

One day, our section was walking along the right hand side of a lane and we were going round a bend when, on another turning ahead of us, was a seventy-ton Tiger tank about 150 yards away. He was so quiet and hardly moving. I don't know who was the most surprised, the tank commander or us, but as soon as he saw us he started to reverse, probably thinking we had an anti-tank weapon, because I was in the lead and was carrying my two-inch mortar. Or probably all he wanted was information concerning our position, since they did not have the spotter planes they had in earlier years. I am pleased he didn't open fire. I don't think I would be sitting here writing now if he had. The tank soon disappeared and I told my officer what I had seen because as he was further back, he had not seen the incident. Soon afterwards, a barrage of heavy fire was laid down upon our area, killing three of our lads, whereupon our officer reported to the commanding officer and very quickly our own heavy guns were giving the enemy more than they had bargained for. Perhaps, after we had reported the sighting, we should have re-deployed.

Later, we advanced over the ground ahead of us and found several Germans dead. For two or three days we just moved forward, sorting out pockets of enemy resistance, killing or taking prisoners. Things were certainly going our way but sometimes at a cost to us in casualties. Nothing of any real significance occurred but we were never free of enemy fire, and we had become so used to it that it didn't bother us unduly. Whenever there was any very feverish activity, our morale still remained high, as it should; the adrenaline quickly flowed as soon as danger threatened. It was an instinctive reaction.

The hedgerows and fairly narrow lanes seemed to go on and on and extreme caution was always essential; a second too slow and you were dead. We carefully turned another bend – these narrow lanes seemed to be all bends – and our lead man observed a German machine gunner behind a tree, his hands still in the firing position, yet there wasn't any movement from him. Taking no chances, we went around the back of him, keeping very low, and saw that he was dead, a knife sticking in his back, his hands still holding his Spandau. He certainly got his just desserts. I reckon he missed the main course!

As we were walking the line of a hedge, I saw some of our tanks moving across a field and suddenly heard the crack of an 88mm anti-tank gun. We had become so used to the sound of German weapons that we knew instinctively what weapon was being fired. Then I saw one of the tanks receive a direct hit and go up in flames, but not before two of the crew came out of the side like jack rabbits. How they bailed out is a mystery. They must certainly have practised that performance during their training.

I had always been of the opinion that our role as infantrymen placed us in the most vulnerable position, but after I saw that tank blown up I was not quite so sure. But unlike us, the tank crews were not continually on Shanks' ponies. We certainly covered some mileage in the PBI (Poor Bloody Infantry!). Our boots were already the worse for wear and our battle dresses were becoming very shabby and dirty.

I went on many patrols during both the evening and at night time (after we had laagered at the end of the day and we had been given a meal of bully stew) looking for signs of the enemy positions. This was when the skills of the attacker were pitted against those of the defender – a cat and mouse game, with possible death as the penalty. The enemy, too, had the same dangerous game to play, keeping tabs on each other's movements at all times.

Strange as it may seem, there was never any shortage of volunteers for patrol. The opportunity to outwit the enemy was a challenge and, linked with the danger, never failed to pump the adrenaline through our veins. It was especially gratifying when we could also collect a few prisoners. We were as good as, or better soldiers than the enemy, and needed to prove it. Sometimes, we lost lads on these patrols and it was always sad.

There was one particular patrol I was on when we ran into trouble. Our section was walking along the back of a hedge for cover when, suddenly, a Spandau machine gun opened up on us from the far corner of the field. Our instantaneous reaction was to dive into the bottom of the ditch, but not before three of our lads were killed. Their bodies were recovered later. After that failed recce we reported, as usual, to our platoon officer, whose response was immediate. I and another lad guided a strong patrol accompanied by two Bren gunners and pointed out where we had got into trouble. Using sign language, we were deployed around the area of the enemy position, with the result that our Bren gunner was able to dispatch the enemy machine gun post, killing two Germans.

I cannot possibly list all our activities in the days that followed, without consulting the history books and that is not my intention. The period was full of activity, during which time we were never far from the sounds of war, much of which was the artillery of both sides. There were many occasions when we came up against some stubborn opposition in the form of a strongly defended farmhouse or a couple of 'hull down' tanks (stationed just below the brow of a hill), when an exchange of fire would develop. At that stage of the war, the eventual result was that the enemy would either be taken prisoner, or liquidated, if they tried to hold out against superior forces.

Whenever we halted, as we did not know how close we were to the enemy, patrols went out to probe the land. On one of these, on 26 June, Corporal Miller went out with six men and was killed by a sniper – poor lad – but we had become so used to seeing sudden death that it did not play on our thoughts for long. We also lost good old Corporal Shaw around this time.

Many prisoners were taken and some of them were Russians who were fighting for Germany rather than go back to Russia. Others were young, fanatical Germans about sixteen or seventeen years of age. Of course, young bodies were lying around all over the place. What a waste.

The enemy was still being very active, which caused us to dig in every time we stopped for a short period, and this meant digging a hole big enough to hide our body using the entrenching tool we all carried with us. If we met any serious opposition, a message would be sent back and help, in the way of planes, tanks, or twenty-five pounder artillery would sort them out, although many times it was up to ourselves to fight it out.

It was now 30 June and we had halted during a lull in the aggression from both sides in the conflict. We spread out, overlooking a field, about four yards apart along one of the ditches which seemed to be never ending. But even when resting we had to be constantly on the alert. From this position, my section was sent on a patrol during daylight at about 1030 hrs and was fired upon by the enemy, so we retraced our steps and made a report to our officer. But it appears that we must have been observed returning to our units because of the shelling which followed.

Half-an-hour later, a pal and I were sitting on the bank of a ditch with out backs to the hedge, having our tiffin, when it happened. We all knew that as long as we could hear shells passing overhead they were not meant for us. If they were, we would not hear them and would not feel much when it happened because it was so sudden. Well, one came over which I didn't hear. The first thing I knew was that I had been thrown into the air and had landed five yards away. I had not felt a thing, but knew that I had been wounded, feeling blood running down my leg, but no pain at all. I had been hit on the inside of my left thigh, very near to you know what! It was incredible how quickly it happened. The blast and shrapnel wounded my pal also. I think how easily I could have been killed. Still, I would not have known anything about it. Somebody called for the stretcher-bearer, which they should not have done in case the sound carried to the enemy.

The first aid soldier came up, tore my trousers off and put a first aid dressing on my wound (everyone carried a large field dressing in a special pocket as part of our battle dress).

The wheels of organisation quickly got moving and in no time at all a four- wheel-drive Jeep came up to the scene and we were both put on a stretcher and fastened to the framework erected on the Jeep for the purpose and away we went. It was a very strange feeling to me at the time. The comradeship in those days was so great among the lads. It is difficult to describe. We were all pals who had together experienced the most traumatic events. We lived together, fought together and sometimes died together, or very often depended upon each other for life itself. We became very close, sharing very emotional times and our officers were included in all our sentiments.

I don't remember whether I was sad or glad that I had been wounded, but I knew that I experienced a great feeling of regret when the Jeep drove across the field and I shouted, 'So long, lads,' and I never saw them again. They were probably thinking, 'Lucky bugger – he is out of it', which, when it comes to the crunch, was true because I could so easily have been killed that day. Now my future lay wherever my fate took me.

I was taken to a field hospital, which was a hive of activity. Well, it would be, wouldn't it? The Royal Army Medical Corps (RAMC) was dedicated to taking care of the wounded. A young lad came and cut my trousers off, then the Medical Officer examined my wound, which was now becoming painful. A large field dressing was put on and I was given a morphine injection and went to sleep.

My last day in the invasion was almost over; I had done my bit. It seemed so long since the first of June, when I had boarded *Empire Lance* at Southampton, the beginning of quite an experience, and I was feeling very tired. I could not remember when I had last had a night's sleep or even taken my clothes off. It had been an experience I would treasure. What I had done and seen would be of immense value in years to come. The events would be my ghosts of the future and I went to sleep.

So ended my part in the invasion. It was 30 June 1944.

Chapter 21

My Rest Cure

A WAY FROM the sounds of the war, I had slept well between white sheets, but as soon as my eyes opened I felt the pain of my wound.

I saw the Medical Officer appear. He was going from bed to bed, asking how we were feeling and giving instructions to the orderlies, one of whom dressed my wound and gave me a morphine injection. I was not feeling too good and another orderly brought me a cup of hot, sweet tea and made me as comfortable as possible. Those orderlies may not have been in the firing line, but they had the skills to do a different kind of job under very difficult circumstances in the field. Sometime during the morning, an ambulance came, took six of us, and headed for the coast.

When I had been wounded, our battalion was in a position near Villers-Bocage, a few miles from the coast, and the trip back to the beaches was slow because the roads were congested with military traffic, mainly the RASC carrying supplies, which had priority, so it took us some considerable time to reach Arromanches, site of the British Mulberry harbour. As I was being transferred to the ship, I felt the ambulance going over the hollow-sounding, floating roadway. As I went over, I was determined to try and have a look at the Mulberry. This prefabricated port was an amazing feat of engineering. Many years later, forty in fact, and the first time I had returned to Normandy, all that remained of that magnificent harbour were the huge blocks of concrete, which will remain for many years to come as a monument to man's genius. My imagination ran wild.

After I had been settled in a bunk, the effects of the morphine and the motion of the hospital ship soon sent me to sleep. I was most surprised when I was awakened to be told that we had arrived at Southampton, from where I had originally sailed to Normandy. It seemed ages ago. Two orderlies carried my stretcher off the ship and put me into one of a fleet of ambulances, which was soon on its way to a Canadian hospital, just outside of Southampton. It was a brand new complex, built for the specific purpose of receiving casualties and was made up of numbers of well-built wooden structures each about twice the size of a Nissen hut, all on ground level. It was situated in lovely countryside and each building was joined by a corridor to the next. It was the 22nd Canadian general hospital and its entire staff were Canadian, devoted to their calling, who treated us all with the utmost care and consideration for our comfort, showing gratitude for what we were, wounded soldiers who had, at first hand, experienced the horrors of war and who now needed their skilled attention.

First of all, I was appointed and introduced to a Canadian orderly. He was a young man named Leslie Buckler. I was put on a blanket-covered couch, then stripped and bathed. All my clothes were thrown into a bin and a new field dressing was put on my wound, which was giving me some pain. They put a nightshirt on me, then took me to a ward and put me into a lovely clean bed with white sheets and pillowcases. To me, it was luxury! It was almost worth being wounded for and a far cry from the fighting of two days ago.

After a short while, a Medical Officer came and examined my wound, which was bleeding again and beginning to cause me some distress. Within one hour, I was having an X-ray to determine the extent of penetration of the shrapnel. I was no sooner back in my bed, than I was out again onto a trolley and given the usual pre-med jab to make me drowsy before being taken to the operating theatre, where a surgeon told me about my wound. At this point, I could not feel my leg at all. Then two bottles were set up, one containing blood, the other with penicillin dripping into my arm. The mask was put over my face and that was all I knew until I woke up. As is usual, after surgery, I didn't quite know where I was and after a little while my orderly came to me and said: 'Well, William Cheall (he'd obviously taken this from my pay book), you are all done and dusted', and then he handed me something wrapped in a bit of gauze for a souvenir. It was the piece of shrapnel recovered from my wound – from an 88mm shell about one-and-a-half inches long and over a quarter-of-an-inch thick. Leslie Buckler asked me if I realised how lucky I had been because the shrapnel – had it hit me one inch higher – would have prevented me from being a parent. When the surgeon came to see me, he said that the piece of steel had penetrated so far into my upper thigh that they had had to put a four-inch cut in my backside to remove it. I still have the shrapnel for a souvenir and also the two scars of my wound.

This was my first contact with the Canadians and I found them to be very efficient and caring. The hospital unit was run entirely by men and my orderly waited on me hand and foot. I have been empathetic towards Canada ever since.

This hospital was only a reception place to sort out various wounded men, so after three days, when I had fully recovered my senses and been given a light meal, no time was lost in putting me in yet another ambulance to a waiting Red Cross hospital train, taking me to goodness knows where. Again, the staff on the train was very caring. Nothing was any trouble and I was soon settled in a bunk so it was great to be molly-coddled. I lay awake, listening, pondering over past events and wondering where they were taking me. Life in the army was like a mystery tour, but usually with more serious consequences!

I was able to talk to the other wounded in bunks near me. Although they were not Green Howards, they were 50th Division lads. Lunch was brought to us and then it was time for a kip. When the stopping of the train woke me up I heard the nurses calling, 'Come on, lads, you've arrived', but there was not a great deal of enthusiasm amongst us. We just waited to see where we were and to be stretchered off the train. We had arrived at Dundee in Scotland and at that time it was a puzzle to me why, given all the hospitals there were in England, they had to send us 550 miles all the way to Scotland.

When I was at Inverary, the previous February, I thought I had seen the last of Scotland. Because of our experiences during the two-week commando course, I was not particularly enamoured with the country. It had never dawned on me then, when I was at the peak of fitness, that I would be returning wounded so soon.

As soon as the ambulance stopped on the forecourt, young Scots girls opened the doors and gave us welcoming smiles. 'Come on lads, cheer up, we will take care of you'. Tucking a blanket around me on a stretcher, they handled me as if I were made of china and took me into Dundee Royal Infirmary, where I was quickly put into a small ward with two other lads. A doctor soon came to my bed and checked my documents and asked me how I felt, after which a nurse gave me a morphine injection and I settled down to sleep. It was 5 July.

Next morning, two nurses – bright and breezy Scots girls – came to my bed, one on each side, and pulled the curtain round and the bedclothes down. No half measures with those girls. They had come to dress my wound and it caused me to be a little embarrassed, but not them. Up with my shirt and there I was almost naked! It was a new experience for me, but I soon got used to it. Then a drip was set up at the bottom of the bed. One nurse held my thigh whilst the other inserted a thick needle which must have been an eighth of an inch thick. I hadn't felt the shrapnel go in because it was so sudden, but I certainly felt that needle! 'There you are, soldier, you will survive'. I was on the penicillin drip for seven days, though after forty-eight hours I was able to sit up at forty-five degrees, but my wound was very painful. It transpired that my two roommates were also from 50th Division and in the Durham Light Infantry. They, too, had been wounded in the legs and were Geordies, from Newcastle. Good lads, the Tynesiders. I had learned long ago how thoroughly reliable and dependable Geordies were. Their temperament was quickly aroused when facing the enemy and they were first-class scrappers.

At the end of seven days, I was put into the main ward where there were thirty other wounded, so there was no shortage of topics of conversation, though they were mostly muted as some of the lads didn't feel inclined to talk and were rather depressed. After losing an arm or leg, or both, who would want to talk his head off?

All the other wounded came from various units of 50th Division, so the conversation was almost all about 50th Division, and their officers, how they were wounded, their experience of D-Day and the days following. I seem to recall that they all thought of their pals who were still fighting in Normandy. Those boys, all around nineteen or twenty years of age, faced a very uncertain future. They had bad dreams about what they had seen and been involved in, calling out during the night. I remember one boy shouting, 'Christ, I've lost my bloody legs!' Then he would wake up and beside the bed would be two of those fantastic nurses, putting an arm round him for comfort.

I now had time to take stock of the situation I had got into. Up until now I had been drowsy all the time. I thought back to the time I was wounded and my experiences since I went on that patrol. I thought about all I had seen since D-Day. It had been an awful experience and I was very lucky indeed to come out of it alive.

Sleep did not come easy during those nightmarish nights. One boy had been blinded and could not accept that he would never see again. What a traumatic transformation for fit, young men to be penalised for the remainder of their lives. I could go on recalling the dreadful wounds I saw. What would these young boys do with their broken bodies? That was the part of war we would all remember. The nurses never seemed to get tired of looking after us. They constantly patrolled the ward, looking at the distress and anxiety in some of the boys' faces.

I looked around me at the other boys in the ward and they were all soldiers who had received all kinds of wounds. One boy opposite me had lost a leg – boy, was I lucky – and he could not accept the fact for days that he only had one leg as he could still feel the missing one. As I said, we were really looked after here. It was my first taste of Scottish hospitality and it was great.

During the night, some of the wounded would moan or groan and shout out. It was really depressing to hear about some of the casualties. Although my wound was bothering me a lot, at least I felt confident that I would make a good recovery, but to lose a limb when one was only around twenty years of age must have been dreadful. It was all so very sad.

The nurses were wonderful and we received almost personal attention. We only had to move and our nurse was beside the bed to tend to our needs. I seemed to have one particular nurse looking after me and, like all the other girls, she was a Scot. She told me that her home was at Dufftown in Banff, about one hundred and sixty miles east of Inverness and she was twenty-one years of age.

Early every morning, two nurses would come to the bed to put me in order and give me a wash. My nurse, Mary Wiseman, would clean up my wound and put on a new dressing then, to my great surprise, she kissed my face. All the girls did this to 'their' boys. I think it must have been part of the recuperation process. When Mary was on duty she always brought me a meal. At night she would tuck me in, give me a kiss and touch my face. Of course, all the boys received the same attention, but I was beginning to think Mary was sweet on me. It was great and I enjoyed the attention. It made me feel good and helped to make my three weeks' stay very pleasant indeed.

Many nights there was not a great deal of sleep for us as some of the boys were dreaming and their nightmares caused them to scream out loud, but this was well-understood by us and they received everybody's sympathy. They were great lads and had made enormous sacrifices for their country.

Before long, I was feeling better in myself. Though my wound still bothered me a great deal, I was able to limp around the ward a little and would make an effort to get some of the badly wounded to come to terms with what had happened to them. But they were in such deep shock, it was beyond my capability to ease their tortured minds. It would take time and, even then, the healing of their broken bodies would be long and in many cases painful.

It had been three weeks since my arrival and the beds were needed for a continuous stream of wounded soldiers, so it was time for me to be moved on. I will always remember the very great kindness and understanding shown to all the lads by the hospital staff during the initial stages of our treatment. As we hobbled onto the forecourt, each nurse gave their boys a kiss and the departure was most touching.

I was now taken by ambulance to a convalescent home. It seemed a long time since I was sitting in the back of a three-tonner on the morning of D-Day although it was only two months since.

Until I went to Dundee, I had never been to Scotland but, of course, I had met Scots men in the army and they were always canny lads. My dealings with the Scots I had met in Dundee confirmed my opinion that they were a generous race of people.

It was a glorious morning travelling through the hills and countryside of Scotland and I was in a very reflective mood. In fact, all ten of us in the truck seemed engrossed with our own thoughts, going over and over the past weeks, totally absorbed about where we had been and where we were going. My immediate future was very certain – I was going somewhere in a three-tonner, my life in the hands of the army! For the past five years, I had been number 4390717. How much longer would it last? It just seemed to go on and on.

I was taken to the village of Killin, and how I would remember that name in years to come. It was situated on the southern end of Loch Tay, in Perthshire. And our new home, Auchmore House, was about one-and-a-half miles from Killin. Until I went to Dundee I had only been to Scotland for training, but of course I had heard all about it from the various Scots lads I had met in the army.

Auchmore House was a large, old residence and in its heyday must have been magnificent and in a way still was, situated in its own extensive grounds. Like the hospital, it was staffed by excellent, caring nurses and we were there to convalesce. It was a rest home for about fifty soldiers and it proved to be a good move being sent here. We were all accommodated in small rooms, and as we were here to recuperate a great deal of leisure time was available, during which we would just read, write or play cards but were free to do almost as we wished, though we had a set routine of light exercises and massaging every day, according to our wounds. But there was a good deal of free time to do as we pleased. There was a well-stocked library, a wireless and a gramophone with a good selection of records. These leisure activities may not seem very exciting but to us lads, who had been used to a strict army routine, they were ideal under the circumstances and they were conducive to recuperation. When I was not reading the books in the library, most of my time was passed making notes and writing of my kaleidoscope of experiences over the past weeks while they were fresh in my mind.

We could walk in the grounds, which were extensive, and I found a huge pine tree, which had been planted by Queen Victoria. I thought, 'To think that I am standing where that great Queen has stood.' The Ink Spots were all the rage, then – better songs than the tuneless stuff they churn out today!

Again, the nurses were fantastic, so kind and generous with their patience and understanding. Two weeks had gone by, when I received a letter which had been posted in Scotland. I have always examined the franking of letters before I open them, but it was Scotland alright and it was from my favourite nurse, Mary Wiseman, wanting to know if she could travel to Killin and stay for the weekend. I had never dreamt of any such thing taking place. Once I had said goodbye at the infirmary, Mary had only remained a lovely memory.

Anyway, I thought, she had been very caring to me and I couldn't possibly have refused. I had a slow walk into the village – the only time I managed it and the furthest I had walked since being wounded. It was also the first time I had seen Killin. The river was flowing fast over the rocks and under the bridge, on its way to Loch Tay; it was soothing to watch. Turning left at the bridge I walked slowly up a slight incline, on one side of which were nice little bungalows. About half way up I chose one with a well cared for front garden. I said to myself, 'This is the one', and wondered if I was being too presumptive about the possibility. Realising I had a bit of a nerve, I knocked on the door and a very motherly lady appeared. I explained how I came to know Mary and that she was a Scot from Banff, and asked if she would let Mary have a room for a night. She replied that she would be only too pleased to help. The room had a beautiful view of the mountains from the window and would be ideal. Facing the front of the bungalow, but a little distance away, the hills rose gently, the guardian of the mountains beyond. It was a picture to delight the eye and a tonic to my recovery.

Mary arrived on the Saturday morning. I hadn't seen her in 'ordinary' clothes before and she looked lovely and was delighted with the place I had chosen for her. Then the lady asked us to have lunch with her at her own table. Over the meal, I explained about the routine of Auchmore and that I was not allowed to stay out overnight and had to be indoors by 10.00 pm. It was a pity that I also had to go back to Auchmore for my treatment but I was back with Mary by 2.30 pm. It seemed that the best thing to do after lunch was to go for a steady walk up the hillside above the bungalow and become acquainted with each other's background. It was a lovely day for just a slow stroll. It would certainly avoid any aggravation to my leg and it was a joy to be holding hands. How could I have ever imagined such a situation not so long ago?

The ground was a mass of heather and bracken and the mountains beyond were just stunning, forming a valley at the bottom of which Killin nestled. How could there be a dreadful war taking place and what would the people of Europe give for such peace and tranquillity? I lay on my back and closed my eyes, saying to myself, 'Thank you, God, for watching over me.' I was carried away by my inner thoughts. Then Mary lay down beside me, putting her head on my shoulder, wanting to know what I was thinking, so I told her of my experiences. She kissed me and said, 'Bill, I love you,' and I squeezed my arm around her. We just lay talking and Mary told me of some of the terribly wounded boys she had been privileged to care for. The truth is we just lay and kissed and cuddled and when I could sense that things might get out of control, I just said, 'Sorry, Mary', and I explained that I was not able to become too involved. My thoughts of the past, present and future dominated all other personal feelings and she, being a country person, understood exactly how I felt. We were two people who could be in control of our mood.

Although I thought that Mary had been growing fond of me while I was in hospital, I had no intention of letting things get out of hand. We just sat and kissed, happy to be in each other's company. We sat up, my arm around her shoulders, silent for a few minutes and I think she greatly appreciated the fact that I had control. From where we sat, with the mountains behind us and the ground in front drifting down into Killin, it was heaven. It was beautiful and we could have sat there forever just looking at the scenery, absorbing every detail. I had a very clear conscience about having upheld my moral principles. I had been reared that way. It was time to go and, holding hands again, we walked quietly back down the hill. When I was in hospital I had thought that Mary was a bit keen on me, but only because of my position as a wounded soldier. It had come as a shock when she told me that she loved me, but although I was very close to returning the affectionate expression, I held back. There was so very much of my life yet to be lived and in my case I was not at all sure what the future held for me.

The weekend had been lovely and memorable, but it had passed only too quickly. I took Mary to her room where I gave her a huge hug, which I hoped said more than words. The kindly lady gave us lunch again, then it was time to go and catch the bus. I did love Mary Wiseman, so it came as no surprise when she told me how she felt towards me. The weekend had been lovely and we walked back slowly down the hill, alongside the rushing river and into the village. I gave Mary another kiss and she climbed onto the bus, shedding a tear. A lovely memory had gone. Had I been kind or cruel?

That was the last time I saw the first love of my life and I haven't forgotten how fate sent me to Scotland, a land of beauty, with lovely Scots lasses.

After the bus left I walked slowly back over the bridge and past the fast flowing river Dochart. I was enjoying the meander back to Auchmore and it gave me time to contemplate the events which had taken place since I went to Dundee. I stood for a while, my thoughts in turmoil about Mary. It had been the first time I had been so close to a girl and I felt a little unsure yet, given all the circumstances, I was of the opinion that I had behaved in a proper manner. I could have so easily pursued this friendship, but the war was still on and I knew I would be going back to my battalion, so this was no time to be thinking of girls. Turning left off the main road out of the village and walking down the wooded lane, I remained a little sad and in deep thought, until I saw the nurses at Auchmore.

It was my birthday, 25 August. Not a soul knew, so it passed just like any other day. After a few days, Mary wrote to me and the gist of the letter was that she wanted to become more involved, but I needed time to think about the correct thing to do.

In case orders came through for us to move on, the nurses at Auchmore paraded all their patients on the forecourt and took photographs: 'Come along, boys, we need snaps of you all before you go.' Small groups of us went to the front of the building where nurses arranged us. They were all treasures and later sent me copies of the snaps. Their kindness knew no bounds and it would be a wrench leaving Killin. Next day, we were issued with new uniforms and knew that we would soon be leaving the paradise called Auchmore.

Before I was posted I thought it best to write to Mary, explaining the dilemma I was in, that although I loved her, we had not known each other long enough to commit ourselves to a relationship. Also, I told her that when my recovery was complete I would be going back to Europe and the war and I could even be killed. I could not make any firm promises, which I knew might have a profound effect upon her life. I never discovered Mary's reaction because she did not reply to my letter. For a long time it was on my mind if I had done the right thing, but common sense prevailed and gradually I accepted it. In the months that followed, whenever I felt in a reflective mood, I often thought of Mary and under the circumstances prevailing at the time I was certain I had acted wisely. It just would not have worked as we could not have spent any time to get to know each other because our homes were so far apart.

I was sorry to leave Killin. The Scotland I had seen in such a short space of time would always remain a treasured memory.

Chapter 22

Back to Duty

TWO DAYS later orders came through for us to get packed and ready to move next day. After breakfast, the nurses, looking rather glum, came round the dining room and gave every one of us a kiss and said goodbye. They had come to know us English boys so well that it was a sad time for them. One or two of the lads who had regained some of their former cheek and bravado, livened up the departure. We climbed into the trucks and were soon on our way. To where? As we left, the girls waved until we were out of sight at the end of the long drive.

Next stop, a complete contrast to Auchmore, was a forbidding-looking place called Glencorse Barracks – even the name seemed ominous. It was a few miles south-west of Edinburgh. It was a formidable, grey-stone building, a typical barrack block with scores of windows overlooking a very large parade ground where, no doubt about it, many a new recruit had been 'broken in' to the ways of that terror of young civilians – the Regimental Sergeant Major! Fortunately, we were far ahead of that ordeal. Anyway, we were only more or less passing through, still on the way to complete recovery from our wounds. A vague and uncertain future lay ahead of us.

I was pleased when I was told to report to a Nissen-hutted camp a quarter of a mile away – the torment of barrack room living was not for us. My first impression of the Nissen camp was that it looked OK, being built on rising ground interspersed with large pine trees, but it was November and Nissen huts in winter were not ideal accommodation, especially after the past four months of the soft life we had lived. 'But this is the army, Mr Jones' as the song goes. Just as well we didn't expect to be there for long; we might even get to like it. But right then there were a few obstacles in the way, in the nature of not-so-good-natured NCOs. They seemed to be more than a little hostile towards us, probably because they knew that we had been part of D-Day and envied us the dubious experience. Or was it because we thought that they had a cushy number, while other soldiers were being put through the mill in Europe? Most likely we did and that they had, but who were we to decide who should do what? Anyway, most of them looked a bit long in the tooth to be fighting Germans. The toughening up process was about to start, and being optimistic that my stay would be short-lived, I did my utmost to become reasonably fit as fast as my wound would allow. My leg was still giving me some trouble and the jagged wound caused by the shrapnel was looking very angry, as was the cut in my backside, so I still had to be careful.

The first thing on the agenda was an examination by the Medical Officer, who said that it was only a matter of time and I would not have any problems. Former wounded soldiers had been assembled here from various convalescent homes and were a mixed bunch of lads from a variety of regiments, and who kept their distance. 'Ah, well, Bill,' I said to myself, 'Be patient, the lads will loosen up. Perhaps their wounds still bother them.' But it was going to take time for them to loosen up.

Happiness evaded me here. It was November, winter, isolated, bitter cold, and discipline was rigid. There was no camaraderie among the men. We were all strangers and the officers had not undergone our experiences, so had no sympathy. We could have been raw recruits there to be trained. It seemed endless and I longed to be back in France, with my company.

Several of the lads had suffered leg wounds of different kinds and severity and we had to go for short steady walks, which gradually increased in length and pace, but fifteen miles was the limit until our legs became stronger. The nearest small town to Glencorse camp was called Penicuik, which was two miles away, and since I had palled up with a Geordie we made several excursions into the town. But back then, in 1944, it was rather a quiet place and since it entailed a four-mile walk we soon stopped that lark. Also, my new pal said that there wasn't any talent there and said, 'Bugger it', or words to that effect. Our next off-duty trip was to Edinburgh, which was ten or twelve miles away. Neither of us had been there before so thought it might be interesting. It was a bitterly cold, second week in December and we decided to go into a little pub in Princess Street for a shandy – it was cheaper than beer and the old problem of financial embarrassment still plagued us.

Two men, they would be in their early forties, came and sat next to us and upon hearing our accent started to chat. As they were Scots, I brought up the fact that I was in 50th Division and that we always fought alongside 51st Highland Division. That really set their tongues wagging and they wanted to know all about the 51st, during which time they bought us a whisky, which almost burnt my throat since I was not a drinker of spirits, anyway. When we said we would have to be going they insisted upon shaking hands and almost in unison asked: 'Tell ye what, laddies, can ye nay come to oor Hogmanay on New Year's Eve?' Well, at that time, I don't think I knew what a Hogmanay was and they laughed and gave us a detailed explanation of what it was all about. It sounded OK to us, but we would need a little time off from camp, which was most likely impossible. We said we would meet the Scots in a couple of days, same pub, same time.

Next day, I spoke to our NCO who seemed to have softened a little towards us. I discovered that he was not a bad sort at heart and he said he would speak to the Captain to try and fix an interview for my mate and me. I was sent for next morning and I told no fibs, just the facts, telling him about the Scots in the pub and I asked if we could be allowed to stay out overnight. He was silent for a while, then suggested that since we were due for a three-day pass anyway, he would grant permission, simply on the grounds that one night off camp would not be enough to recover from a Hogmanay and were we sure we knew what we were doing? We had found a chink in the rigid routine at Glencorse; it was not so bad, after all!

We made the trip into Edinburgh to meet our two friends, who arranged to pick us up outside our camp during New Year's Eve, which they did. We first went to the same little pub for a drink, where the atmosphere was warming up ready for the festivities. The drink over, our host took us to one of their houses, where we were introduced to his wife. As the evening wore on, more folk turned up, just enough to make a sociable gathering. We were the only foreigners present and some wanted to know about us. Just to mention the 51st and 50th Divisions pleased them enormously. To cut a long story short, by the time it was midnight we were just a teeny-weeny bit so-and-so, but not too far gone to hold hands and sing Auld Lang Syne. What happened after that I hadn't a clue.

The mood of everybody was marvellous; all those Scots taking us two English lads to their hearts, and they looked after us for the three days, then took us back to camp. I had a very strong feeling that our Captain knew all about Hogmanay! It was now 1945.

Back at our camp we both soon came back down to earth. The routine was still the same, with the aim of making our recovery complete, but it did not last long. Two weeks later a move came about, and from the start it proved to be a good one. Since I had only had the one three-day pass since early May (in eight months), I went to the orderly room to enquire what the chances were of a leave before the move came about and they agreed. Next day, I collected my rail warrant and ration card for seven days' leave. At the same time, I was given a rail warrant, which would take me from my home to my new base. I was astonished to find that it was Bridlington on the east coast, and only seventy miles south of my home. I knew Bridlington well.

I was taken by fifteen-hundredweight truck to Waverley Station with all my kit, and I felt happy going on my first leave since well before D-Day. There would be so much to talk about. I looked forward with very pleasant anticipation to a few days with my family and friends. It would be many years before I rediscovered the beauty and memories of Scotland.

So I found myself speeding on a train to Bridlington. When I arrived at my new posting, I discovered that it was a holding unit, mainly to make sure we were fit enough for further active service whenever the need arose. I was a shadow of my former self, but at least my mental attitude to events had been retained and I would put every effort into regaining some semblance of my fitness prior to the invasion.

Our billets consisted of requisitioned private hotels on the outskirts of the town, a couple of hundred yards from the sea front. We each had a single metal bed, three to a room. The first thing on the agenda was a medical parade to assess our state of health which proved to be quite an experience, since we were all single young lads. We fell in on the road outside and entered the building in single file, then stripped naked, each man carrying his own clothes. We had done this many times over the years and thought nothing of it, until the Medical Officer appeared – a female doctor, about twenty-five years of age. Nurses had seen me naked many times when I was wounded and at Dundee, but for most of the lads it was a new experience, and judging by the comments afterwards, they enjoyed being fondled by a female doctor!

We started to undergo training within a week, the same almost basic training I had done years previously and we all became friendly. Many of the lads had not seen active service as this was a holding battalion and would supply soldiers to active service units when they needed replacements for casualties. Before I was wounded, I was at the peak of fitness with mental attitude to match. I now needed, more than anything, the stimulus of more energetic activity and there was a lack of sufficient intelligent activity to occupy our young minds. The worst possible thing for a soldier is to be undergoing the same routine, day after day, requiring no thought or physical effort. That was the routine at Bridlington, and the lads were browned off. I decided that at the first opportunity I would volunteer to return to Europe, from where I had been ejected so suddenly by a piece of shrapnel which would change what remained of my life in the army.

Although most of these lads had been wounded in the Normandy fighting, many of them had not experienced the trying conditions during long route marches and winter exercises, as at Inverary, to toughen them up, and none of that was forthcoming. It would be unwise to send them back to Europe in the physical condition they were in, and everybody did expect to go back into action at some point.

The best thing about Bridlington was that we had a proper NAAFI, which was situated in what had been the pier restaurant, and where we could go during time off for a penny cup of tea and to talk to a girl across the counter. They were good girls, who tolerated none of the crude behaviour of some of the lads, whose talk and behaviour could at times be questionable. But when it came down to the nitty-gritty, they were good lads. They all still belonged to their original regiments. I was the only Green Howard and still had my GH insignia. We were certainly a mixed bag.

Many of them were interested to know how I came to be one of them, after I had served at Dunkirk, North Africa and Sicily, then Normandy. As the only action they had been involved in was Normandy, they pressed me to tell them about the other theatres of war. I often wondered how I had been lucky enough to survive. I was wishing I was with my old battalion, where we were all on the same level. For the first time I came into contact with lads from London, but not Cockneys. I palled up with one of them, called Tommy Chaffe, who was younger than me. I used to laugh at his accent and his manner; it was so different to the northerners I had always served with. He had never been in action and was just waiting to be posted.

I was just about fed-up with the mind-boggling routine, when a list was put on the notice board giving names of lads to be on a draft; everyone knew it had to be Europe and nobody cared. As far as I was concerned there was only one problem. I was not on the list, but my new pals were, and I was fed up, so I thought hard about it then asked for an interview with the company commander and explained my dilemma. He understood how I felt. When I asked to be included in the draft, my request was granted. I remember the anticipation of hoping that I would once again be joining the old 6th Green Howards. It was not until after the war that I learned that at the time I volunteered, the 6ths had been taken out of the line after advancing as far as Nijmegen in Holland. They were battle-weary and had returned to England, and were stationed at Malton in Yorkshire in December 1944. Had I been aware of it, my decision to volunteer would certainly have been in doubt. However, in the end, things did turn out well for me.

After seven days' leave, I reported back to Bridlington, after which time we were soon on our way to Germany. It was February 1945. Although I didn't know it then, that move was responsible for my meeting the girl I married.

Chapter 23

Hamburg and Peace

THE WAY the war was going at the time (it was March 1945) surely it could not go on for much longer. Or so we thought, but that possibility had entered our minds many times over the past months and it still went on and on. We could never tell with the Germans. They had lost the war, that was obvious, but their leaders would not surrender the total power they had over the whole population. Although the older generation German soldier seemed resigned to his fate when captured, the younger Hitler youth fought with tenacity, and when captured showed a great deal of arrogance.

During the third week of March, we had a kit inspection in readiness for our departure at the end of the week. The remainder of the day was free to do as we wished, but was spent writing letters or playing cards. Things were so different in those days. There was very little drunkenness or extreme bad behaviour among the lads. I know they used a lot of bad language and fantasised about girls, but at heart, the British soldier was a good sort of chap and talk about girls stimulated their imagination.

There were about fifty men on the draft and there was still speculation about where we were going. Once again, three-tonners were used to take us to Dover and via a very buoyant sea to Ostend, though we had no chance of seeing anything of the place because we transferred off the ships straight onto trucks – from which vantage point we could return the waves of the civilians as we passed through their town – on the way to what proved to be a delightful place, Brugge in Belgium.

Unfortunately, the war was still going on and our thoughts were not really attuned to admiring scenery, but more to what lay ahead of us. We were billeted in a rather barn-like building, all timber, but situated almost in the centre of the town. For the first time ever I found myself, even if only for a short while, billeted in a town centre. Brugge seemed to have recovered, at least on the surface, from the effects of occupation, but it would take years before the mental scars disappeared. The effects of the ruthless occupation, for almost five years, must have taken a dreadful toll on their way of life. The shops, although showing signs of neglect (I noticed this because of my pre-war business experience) had made some progress in bringing an appearance of normality into their various trades.

Photographers were on the streets doing brisk business among servicemen, making capital out of the fact that friendly forces had arrived in their midst. They were probably just as enthusiastic when the enemy were amongst them – after all, business is business – but I'll wager they fleeced the unsuspecting Germans. I could not understand why we had been sent to Europe. Instead of going to the front we had been billeted in a lovely city, but we were not complaining, just curious. We had ample time to explore the long walks and waterways and to admire the splendid town hall.

I then suffered a bitter disappointment. I was not to rejoin my old battalion, but had been unknowingly transferred to the East Lancashire Regiment. Me, a proud northern lad of the Green Howards, finding myself posted to a Lancashire Regiment! At the time I was extremely put out; I had been looking forward to seeing all my old pals of the 6th, supposing they had all survived the battles taking place after I had been wounded. Even though my cap badge had changed twice to other regiments, I was always a Green Howard at heart. How would I adapt to a Lancashire regiment? I would have to wait and see.

The whereabouts of the East Lancashires was quite unknown to me. We were told they were, 'Somewhere in Germany', which was very vague and nobody told us what to expect. Once again, we were only numbers in the infantry.

We stayed at these barracks, sleeping on straw for four days, just waiting and waiting. Nobody seemed to know anything about what was happening at the front and we did not have any newspapers now.

During the third week of April, we packed our kit for yet another move, as we thought, towards the action. No-one ever told us how the war was going and no radio was available, and the worst of it was that nobody seemed to know what to do with us. We travelled northeast through the flat countryside of Holland and were soon upon a scene so familiar to those brave men of the paratroops – Arnhem, the graveyard of many brave young men and of Market Garden itself. The slender hold the paras had on their positions was impossible to sustain. Everything had been against them, except their own determination and bravery, to try and hold on and make the enemy pay very dearly, until help could arrive, but it had been in vain. The help never arrived and the operation failed. That was the countryside we passed through. Broken gliders, smashed Jeeps and equipment and all the paraphernalia of a stubborn and grim battle lay everywhere throughout the once-lovely countryside. What very sad and bitter memories the survivors, many of them crippled, would have to come to terms with; to never forget what at the beginning must have been a well-planned attack, but which went wrong.

About three miles further on we came to a halt at some large barns on a Dutch farm. We were to stay here for the night, sleeping on the straw which covered the ground, but first a good meal had been brought up to us and then guards, including myself, were placed at intervals around the area.

During the dark hours, as I walked about on guard, my imagination ran riot about what must have happened at Arnhem and in the skies above me, not so long ago. It was almost impossible to believe that a catastrophe had taken place and how very disillusioned those paratroops must have been to find the enemy so strangely entrenched, yet so soon after the inquest about the operation it was now part of history. The two hours on guard and four hours off passed quickly.

We had to be up early and were feeling dishevelled, having slept with our clothes on, but a quick cold wash and shave soon livened us up. After we'd had breakfast, we collected our small pack, which contained our personal things. Our rifle never left our sides. If our kit was stolen, that was one thing, but our rifle was something else. After a roll call, we climbed aboard our trucks and continued on our way, still not knowing a thing about what was happening, just like so many parcels being delivered; why couldn't somebody tell us something? We were completely in the dark, until the next day.

We came to a halt in a clearing and an officer from the East Lancs addressed us, saying that negotiations were taking place about a cease-fire. Another roll call took place and then the officer explained to us about our joining the East Lancashires, and assigned us to different companies of the 1st battalion. Then, surprise, surprise, we were actually told where we were – near Hamburg, which we could see in the distance.

We stayed in those positions overnight, just sleeping on our groundsheets. It seemed so eerie to me and everything was so quiet. When last time I was in Europe the sounds of war were very near. I couldn't believe the possibility that it could soon be all over. Many times in the past, it had seemed that it would never end and now what we had waited for so long was on the verge of becoming reality. Next morning, after making ourselves presentable, we queued for breakfast then enbussed. We were going to meet our new battalion. I knew from the start that I would be continually comparing it with the Green Howards. The faces of a great number of them still lingered in my memory and it would feel strange for a while.

We joined the battalion and took part in a few actions clearing the enemy out of strong points. Then we crossed the River Elbe on a pontoon bridge which the engineers had put across. Hamburg fell without a great deal of hassle – the Germans were on their last legs.

I decided, now the war had ended, to settle down in my new regiment. I had survived. I had peace of mind, and knew that it was only a matter of time before I would be going home to a life I had left so many years ago. I was now Bill Cheall 4390717 HQ Company, 1st Battalion, The East Lancashire Regiment, and bound for a new experience. We were given a talk about out responsibilities and conduct towards the civilians and then the order came for us to move forward and take up occupation duties.

We were never told that the war had reached an end. It was just another day, and everywhere was so quiet as we finally came to rest on the outskirts of Hamburg.

We then joined the companies to which we had been assigned. It puzzled me as to why I had been placed in the Headquarters Company. Perhaps it was down to the fact that at some time in the past, which seemed years ago, I had been a cook, and had also been Number One on the mortar. The boys just talked to each other about what might happen now. Though nobody expected to be going home tomorrow, they were only too pleased that the danger had gone and that all we had to do was our duty as it was explained to us. There were no celebrations, whatsoever, not even a drink – nothing – to celebrate the end of such an evil catastrophe as the Second World War. To think that after all these years of fighting for our country it was all over. It was almost uncanny!

I decided to put every effort into my activities in my new regiment. The billets of HQ Company were ex-council buildings which had escaped any serious damage during the bombing. Just across the road, but at 9 o'clock from our billets, there was another large property in perfect condition, and it extended for about forty yards down to a large lake.

The building had been the home of the Gauleiter of Hamburg and he certainly seemed to like comfort. The place was fully furnished and untouched by the war. I went into the house and found several things of interest for souvenirs; a seven-inch dagger decorated with a swastika and tassel, a very large, swastika flag; boxes full of medals, but no Iron Crosses. I ventured into a room, about fifteen meters square, which had shelves around all the walls laden with brand new linen of all kinds – bed clothes, towels and everything to do with a large household – just left when the occupants had fled. Another room, which must have been an office of some kind, was fully equipped as such, with a solid oak desk and many cabinets, all full of stationery. The whole house was magnificently appointed. I think the Gauleiter and his staff must have been Nazis because they had fled before we arrived.

Before I settled down for the night, I thought of the many things which had happened to me during my war, and how I had been fortunate enough to have survived. For some time, it was very hard to accept that the war was over. The sound of heavy guns and mortars, bombing and sniper fire had gone, as had the death-dealing mines. Also, the constant awareness that some of our lives could be snuffed out in a split second, the killing and murdering of civilians and the occupation of the downtrodden countries. Now it was all over and at the end it was we who were going to do the occupying. It was the responsibility of the East Lancs, in our sector, to keep order but in a peaceful manner. We had to adapt to an entirely new way of life. No more military exercises or thirty-mile marches. Who cared if a Bren gun weighed twenty-two pounds? Never again would it press into our shoulders when it was our turn to carry it. D-Day was eleven months behind us but the memories would be with us far into the future.

We were the first soldiers in our part of Hamburg and being rather towards the outskirts, it was not too badly damaged. Yes, we did the occupying all right. To start with, a patrol consisted of nine men – one section and an NCO – carrying loaded rifles just in case of any public demonstration. We would walk around our designated area and after a while the patrol consisted of only two soldiers.

The German civilians, mainly older men and women and young children (the older children had been drafted into some kind of war effort) seemed to be utterly dejected and downtrodden. Everybody looked weary and hungry, unable to imagine how this could be the end of all the mighty power the German war machine had wielded in the past. These were the people who had shown no mercy to anybody standing in their way. They must have been suffering mentally as well as physically, under their tyrant masters because of the terror tactics employed by the Gestapo.

I wondered if they expected sympathy and understanding from us, unlike the Gestapo's lack of compassion for the subjugated peoples of Europe. But the Allies were different. We were not there to browbeat the German people and there would not be any intimidation on our part. We would do our job in a correct and peaceful manner and that is how we went about it.

No resentment was shown towards us and they accepted their fate unquestionably. They had lost the war and were pleased to see the end of it, so accepted the conditions of peace. The laws we worked under were strict. Under no circumstances were we allowed to even try to make conversation with them. We just went about our duty quietly and purposefully, letting them see by an uncaring attitude towards their fate that they deserved all they had got. I felt that they could not understand why we made no attempt to converse with them. But, and it was a large but, we were not by nature, the aggressive and heartless bullies which the SS had turned out. We were very perceptive and sympathetic in our approach to a very delicate situation. There was a very noticeable absence of boys and men who, of course, had all been absorbed into the defences. After a while, our army command relaxed the fraternisation ban and under special circumstances our lives were made a little easier to conduct when we could, if necessary, make a gesture of almost friendliness towards the people.

The 1st Battalion, East Lancashire, was a Regular Army unit and would be expected to perform duties wherever the War Office decided to send them, but at present there were very few full-time servicemen in the battalion. It consisted almost wholly of soldiers like myself who had been called up, probably become a casualty and sent to a holding battalion. There was a great preponderance of Territorial Army and conscripted men. Given those conditions, the 1st Battalion comprised men from most parts of the country, not just Lancashire

About four weeks after I joined the regiment – it seemed so strange to me – I was issued with a cap badge, shoulder flashes and divisional signs. It was now official. I was no longer a Green Howard. Almost at the same time, I received a most welcome letter from home, which contained a very pleasant surprise, a wound stripe and more importantly, my Eighth Army ribbon, which had been sent by the War Office. I felt like a dog with two tails because I was proud to have been in Monty's Eighth

Army. I had a right to be proud, too. I had not up to that time seen any other East Lanc wearing that special ribbon. After I had 'put it up' the lads wanted to know where I had been in the Middle East.

Two days after I had sewn on my ribbon, I was passing my company commander and after returning my salute he asked me to wait a moment, then asked me my name. Next morning, I was told by the Sergeant Major that the Company Commander wanted to see me in his office at 1300 hrs. I duly went and he asked me about my service. At the end of the interview, he asked that as I was a senior soldier, would I care to join the Regimental Police, with the rank of Lance Corporal. I didn't have to give an immediate answer but could let the Sergeant Major know the next day. I did think about it and wondered how it would affect my relationship with the lads. I had never sought promotion, had always put the comradeship of the lads first and felt I might jeopardise the friendship I had always enjoyed with the other ranks. But the war was over now and for a change I had to look at things in a different light. I had a disturbed few hours, then made my mind up to accept the police position. I had always been conscientious and knew that I could adapt to any given situation that I might find myself in as a consequence of this. I never regretted it.

I put up my stripe and felt rather proud and wondered if I had been missing something over the past years, when I could so easily have had promotion. But that was the past. Think of the present, Bill. To my surprise and delight, I took delivery of a BSA 250cc motorcycle, crash helmet and revolver and a pamphlet about the work of the police. When I took delivery and rode it for the first time, I thought of when I was at Dunkirk and found the baked beans in the back of the ambulance. How the time had flown!

I moved out from my mates, hoping that they would always remember our friendship, and joined three other lads who had also been selected to join the police. They came from other companies and we soon swapped our experiences. All were determined to succeed in making the new police a success. We had been given the authority and we all shook hands. I knew that we would make a good team.

I soon felt that I had found a good niche for myself in the East Lancs and devoted my thoughts and energy to the job I had been entrusted with. It was a very responsible position, which would keep me fully occupied mentally and physically. For that I was thankful. On my first patrol I felt a little strange driving around the area designated to the battalion, wearing my white webbing and gaiters. The two-man army patrol had now been suspended. The police were responsible and the civilians seemed to accept our presence without any sign of being resentful.

One day I was riding along a road past a cemetery and there was a wide grass verge and what appeared to be an empty, mass grave which was almost freshly dug – it was about eight feet deep and sixty feet long. What a way to be buried. I wondered if it had been prepared for victims of the mass bombing of Hamburg, which had caused so many deaths.

When the fraternisation ban was lifted, it was much more agreeable to be able to pass a civil word to people who would say the odd word of greeting, but in English of course. I never got close enough to them to be able to learn any of their language, except the time of day. Most instructions I had to give during the course of my duties were given in sign language and I did not have any problems in that respect. They had been our bitter enemies for too long to be forgiven so quickly. It would have to be seen whom the victors were without any signs of aggression on our part and that is how we behaved, going about our responsibilities quietly and purposefully.

One of the consequences of being allowed to mix with the public – even to have a drink in their pubs – was that some of the lads got carried away and became attracted to the opposite sex and after a period of time paid the penalty by catching that dreadful disease we all knew about. The married men amongst them were the first to complain if somebody informed them that their wives were misbehaving. That situation arose many times during the war. Then a soldier would be granted compassionate leave and after returning would once again seek the opposite sex to do what he had condemned his wife for. What a life! If the powers that be had given any thought to the matter, our lads would have been issued with the necessary item for safer sex, as the American servicemen were.

During my service I had to attend several courts martial of soldiers who had gone absent without leave; the usual reason being that they had become acquainted with a fräulein, or frau for that matter, and could not resist the usual temptation of taking up residence. The Military Police usually caught up with the miscreant and arrested him. The appropriate unit was then informed and the Regimental Police would escort them back to their battalion HQ. I went to Düsseldorf on several occasions for that reason. The usual punishment for AWOL for any length of time would be a term in the 'glasshouse' (military prison) and that was no soft option as was well known.

I visited Hamburg several times on duty and the destruction was unbelievable with a complete collapse of large areas. Hamburg, alone, paid the penalty for the suffering of Coventry. It had been avenged.

There was never a dull moment for me and there was always interesting work to be done. One of the most distressing of those tasks took place over a period of three full days. The police had to accompany six officers on a very unpleasant duty, but at the same time giving us first hand insight into what had taken place in Germany over the past years. We went to a large field about four miles from our billets, and what we saw had to be seen to be believed. There were literally many thousands of displaced persons standing around with vacant, hungry looks upon their faces, waiting for somebody to guide them and to tell them what was being done to help them. There were other people, half-witted because of their experiences. None of them seemed to know where their families were; all were undernourished, underclothed and altogether a tragic sight. Those poor souls had been uprooted from their homes and families forcibly, from all over the occupied territories, and made to contribute every sinew in their bodies to the German war effort, by their forced labour in the factories.

We set up trestle tables and an officer, together with a linguist who spoke several languages, sat at each table. We police had to keep order and organise the poor souls into single file to wait their turn to seek a solution to an extremely difficult problem. It was all done by signs on our part because of the many languages involved, but that was no problem since most of them were docile, being well-behaved, and just stood there wondering what on earth was to happen to them, as if in a trance. I was at a table all day, for three days, listening to the very patient officers asking questions, all beyond my comprehension. I thought how marvellous it was to be a linguist, watching those clever men, with their voices and signs, trying to get to the bottom of so many problems.

The people came from so many different countries and to me it looked an impossible task. Those people wanted to return to the homes which they had been forced to leave, but it was easier said than done. Their minds must have been in torment. It was a monumental task which had to be done as quickly and humanely as possible but, meantime, they had to be fed and protected against any one of them who had gone berserk. We had to show sympathy, kindness, firmness and above all, understanding of the needs of those poor individuals who longed to get back to the folk they expected to find waiting for them. What a tremendous upheaval of humanity the Nazi regime had brought about in their determination to subjugate the once great nations of Europe. It was a marvel that it was ever sorted out, but for many a poor soul it never would be.

Being a witness to what happened over those three days was something I will never forget. But for that heaving mass of tragic humanity who paid the penalty with their mental and physical suffering it would be an almost unbelievable burden, which they would take to their graves. The Allies did a monumental job here and the countries should be forever grateful.

I was pleased I had joined the Regimental Police because my duties enabled me to see, first-hand, the aftermath of war in Germany, which I would otherwise never have seen, or even believed. I also came to realise that not at all Germans wanted the war with all the consequences which had been forced upon them by a ruthless and heartless dictatorship.

Chapter 24

Oberhausen, Germany

I THINK to reduce the risk of boredom, soldiers were moved around very often, hopefully not giving them time to become too well acquainted with a given area. Therefore, during the first week of August 1945, a move became imminent and within three days became a fact. We had packed up, ready to abandon our first comfortable billet for many a long time.

Travelling again by road, through the war-torn countryside of Germany gave us first-hand knowledge of the way the Germans had been brought to justice and made to suffer. We ended up at Oberhausen, in the Ruhr district of Germany, quite a way from Hamburg. Whereas Hamburg had been a prosperous area, Oberhausen, because of its position in a great industrial basin, was more working class, but nevertheless it had been prosperous, though not anymore, because of the destruction.

We were billeted in what seemed to have been makeshift offices belonging to the IG Farben chemical company. The firm's name was on a tall tower about fifty yards away, which had miraculously escaped being destroyed during the bombing. I gathered the impression that all the remaining works buildings were a temporary affair, replacing those which had been destroyed. Nothing looked permanent, except a main office block which, apart from the windows, was untouched.

Before our billets were occupied, I accompanied our officer on an inspection of the place. Can you imagine our surprise when, upon opening a locked cupboard, we found a full case of twelve bottles of Scotch whisky, in Dimple bottles? The officer's eyes lit up and he said, 'Hell, Cheall, what a find.' He then handed me a bottle and took the remainder to share with the other company officers. My bottle went home with me when I later went on leave.

After the company had settled in, the orderly room sent for me and informed me that a course had been set up at Düsseldorf for regimental police and that I was to go on it, being the senior soldier among the police. The course proved to be a great revelation to me. The Military Police organised proceedings and I was taught the theory and practice of policing in an occupied country, what to do in different situations, how to treat the civilians under difficult conditions and how to handle any emergency which might arise. I even did a stint of traffic control on the main street of Düsseldorf. It was all most interesting and I also developed a different attitude towards the Red Caps, who had never been popular with the other ranks.

While I was on the course, discipline amongst us was enforced. The course was intended to stimulate our respect for army law and to uphold it in a conscientious manner in a very difficult environment. We did have certain times off during the evenings and three of us, for safety, used to walk along the riverside, go into a pub and have a glass of weak beer, chat about the course and also about the regiments we had been in before joining the East Lancs. The civilians in the place always greeted us cordially. Whether they really meant it was something else. We had been issued with a complete new outfit of clothing and were looking really smart as we walked about. Most of the German frauleins gave us lingering looks, but our behaviour had to be impeccable at all times. We could be friendly to a certain extent but had not to show any weakness in our conduct.

The two weeks at Düsseldorf soon passed because our time was almost fully taken up with a comprehensive daily schedule. It proved to be most interesting and it was a stimulating challenge to show that we could do the job we had been selected for. During the journey back to Oberhausen, in an army workhorse – the fifteen-hundredweight truck – the driver said: 'Tell you what, Bill, we will go a bit out of our way. I want to show you something.' We went through what had been Essen and compared to the destruction there, Hamburg had been fortunate (and that city had been raised to the ground!). Hardly anything had been left standing and whole areas had been blasted into heaps of rubble. Essen had been a very important part of the German economy, so crucial to their war effort, that the Allies making it a prime target had destroyed its potential. I saw a large twisted sign leaning against a pile of rubble, which had been a factory. It said, 'Alfred Krupp'. I wondered how many Tiger tanks had been turned out from there. Yes, and steel to make the dreaded 88mm guns, which had caused so many problems in battle to our lads. They certainly got more than they had bargained for at Essen. It pleased me enormously to see it and to remember it. It was a pity Hitler didn't live to see the results of his madness.

Now it was back to duty and I had to report my return to the orderly room, where funnily enough I got the impression that the NCOs showed a little more respect than one usually received from the battalion orderly room. It made me more determined than ever to be a good policeman.

We continued to do patrols on our motorbikes and to be frank it was becoming enjoyable. The days had gone when there was any possibility of resentment towards our presence. The population had suffered the first shock of defeat and were now accepting what they could not possibly have foreseen in the heyday of their country.

The companies of the battalion were spread out over a large area and it was my duty to cover that area, which involved having to cross an excellent pontoon bridge across the River Elbe at Duisburg. It was a marvellous feat of engineering. The engineers were very clever doing the work they did on the Bailey bridges. Duisburg, too, had been a prime target of the air force.

I had been back from my course about a week when my company commander wanted to see me and told me that the result of my police course was very satisfactory. Consequently, I was being promoted to the rank of full Corporal and would be in charge of the Regimental Police. I was very pleased at the opportunity and responsibility I had been given, and the challenge was something I knew I could cope with.

Since we had begun the occupation, I think the men of the companies had shown signs of boredom, mainly through the lack of anything constructive to do to use up the reserves of energy, rather than spending so much time almost lazing around. It was not the same as being billeted in an English town, where one could always find something to do. At Oberhausen, or any other German town near us, there weren't any opportunities to relieve the boredom. The lads passed much time playing cards, reading, or listening to the radio, particularly Vera Lynn. At least I had my police duties to keep me mentally stimulated, not the least of which was keeping myself clean and well turned out. I can recall travelling on the trains, which were absolutely packed with civilians.

One evening, I was sitting in my room alone, thinking how good things had turned out for me and I started to sing the songs of the day, when suddenly there came a tap on the door and a sergeant walked in and asked if it was me who had been singing, so I said it was.

'Right, I am putting on a bit of a show for the lads, they are feeling browned off.' After a pause, he went on: 'And I am hoping that you will give us a couple of songs. How about it, Bill?' It seemed I hadn't got any alternative, so I agreed. A week later, the proposed 'bit of a show' became a reality and although I was a touch nervous, I stood there and sang what I knew the lads wanted to hear and made them a little sad thinking of home and families, but much of the time they all joined in the singing and the show went off well. I sang, 'We'll meet again', and 'You'll never know' with some of the other lads doing their bit. Perhaps I put more into my singing because I was going on leave shortly! That reminds me; somewhere at the back of my mind there are many memories which I can recall so vaguely that I cannot get a sufficient grasp of things to write about them, but they are there, tucked away so deeply in my thought that they will remain there and die with me. That leave is one of them. I can't recall a single detail!

Back in England, sometime after the war ended, I was driving into the nearest town to where my village was and I saw an amazing coincidence on a road sign, 'Middlesbrough, twinned with Oberhausen.' How strange it seemed to me at the time – a constant reminder to me of my time there.

Chapter 25

Duisburg, The End of My War

A T THE end of September, it was time for the company to be on its way to pastures new – though not so much pastures as rubble – to be more central and accessible to the other companies.

Just about three miles or so south of Duisburg, we turned right off the main road and travelled along a narrow winding lane for nigh on a half mile and came upon this wonderful oasis on the left. It had a typical German name, 'Wolfsburg'. In earlier days it must have been a kind of country club and there was an empty swimming pool at the rear. The mansion, which is what I would call it, was set in a large, lawned, area among trees and was like something out of a fairy tale. Such a building might be seen in Scotland. It looked magnificent and reminded me of Inverary Castle even down to the pointed towers. It looked a picture and I recall it many times in my memories.

This was to be our company headquarters and it had been left with everything intact. Some top men must have lived there. It seemed to me that at some time it had been a gentleman's country club and it was immaculate.

There was a canteen, which was a luxury we had never had before, and to be able to sit for our meals was most agreeable since, as a rule, we either sat on anything available or just stood. At Wolfsburg, I usually sat at the same table as a lad called Harold Greenwood I had formed a friendship with. He had been on guards and I too was doing my rounds, checking security. Lads soon became comrades in the army. Funny thing about Harold; he always made a meal of his fingernails whenever we met in the canteen for a chat, but he was a good sort and we got on well together. He came from Darwen in Lancashire. I could never understand why he smoked so much, but then, so did most of the lads. Thinking about it, going back to my earlier comment about boredom, the lads did have far too much time on their hands. In earlier times, there had always been a full programme of training, but in Germany, after the end of the war, there was no doubt about it, the lads were bored and could light up whenever they felt the need of what we now know is a dreadful addiction. Harold died from lung cancer some years later, at the age of 51. It is strange how one's life can be governed by a friendship. The year after I was demobbed, my pal was on leave from Germany and I went to Darwen to see him and his family, and to cut a long story short, directly through Harold and his sister I met the Lancashire lass, Anne, who became my wife, and he married Anne's best friend, Florence. God works his wonders in a mysterious way. I wonder what my life would have been had I not joined the East Lancs.

About a month after we had moved to Wolfsburg, it became obvious that the police were too close and were getting too familiar with the lads, so we had to move, and although I was not pleased at the time there was nothing I could do about it. The officers, who had lived in the same building, also moved out. The new officers' quarters and the battalion orderly room were only about three hundred yards from Wolfsburg.

There was a small cottage where the police lived, a short distance away, which looked as though it could have been the lodge of the estate and it was perfect. We each had our own room and there was an outhouse where we kept our motorbikes. There was also a small, well-kept garden. It was in a lovely spot. I can see it now; the little greenhouse and the sweet corn, just left to rot. Again, the civilians had fled.

At the front of the new battalion HQ there was a large circular lawn inside a gravelled driveway and in the centre of the lawn there was a flag pole from which we flew a large Union Jack. I felt ever so proud when, as duty officer, I raised the flag every morning and in the evening lowered it and saluted. It gave me an incredible feeling inside, which one rarely felt in the army. To think that the swastika used to hang there and the flag of the victors had taken its place; a very conscious memory for me.

One thing about the Germans was that they were good organisers and one day the Duisburg authority decided to hold a sports meeting. How quickly things got moving. Our police were ordered to attend the meeting to make sure nothing untoward was taking place, but all the civilians by that time had accepted their lot and were most sociable and showed no sign of resentment towards us. It was a great, sunny day out and I think it was a very good thing that we were given the opportunity of mixing more with the population and it helped to alleviate the routine of life in the army

At the beginning of December, our company commander thought it would be good to give a Christmas party to about one hundred German children of about nine years of age. When the day arrived, they were assembled in the school hall and the police were present to give a hand. The looks on the children's faces were a just reward for the effort put into the party. They had never seen such a spread in their young lives. Food had been short in Germany for years and it was good to see them all so happy. At the end, a teacher told them all to stand and thank our officers. Then the teacher standing at the front raised her arms for attention, gave some instructions and the children all started to sing their national carol, Silent Night. We were all very touched; it sounded so beautiful. I was so impressed that every year I think of those German school children in that schoolroom near Duisburg.

The memory is so vivid that in December 1986, forty-one years after the occasion, I wrote to the information bureau at Duisburg, telling them of my experience and asked if there was a record available of German children singing Silent Night and if they would send it to me, letting me know how much money I should send back. They replied, sending the record I had requested, with English and German words on an enclosure. It was a very kind letter, which I have kept. They thanked me for sharing my memories with them. It was signed by Dietmar Wolf and the record was a gift from the German people. I can't express in words my feelings, sufficient to say that every Christmas I play the record, recalling that lovely day in 1945.

Part of our battalion was still billeted in Oberhausen and the area round about. Almost every day I had to visit one or another of them with orders of one kind or another. Yes, it was a good move becoming a policeman and a very respectable position to be in. I was also held in a certain esteem because I had the honour to be able to wear the Eighth Army ribbon with a tiny eight in the middle of it, of which there were very few in my company. None of the officers had served under Montgomery.

News of demobilisation began to come through and we all waited to see when we were going to be released. All the older regular soldiers who were serving before the war started would go first, then chaps like me who were called up on 24 August 1939.

It set me thinking about my own position. When the time came, it seemed almost fantasy that the end was in sight and now it was near I was not so sure I welcomed it. I began to wonder if I should sign on as a regular soldier because the East Lancs experience had been good for me. There was never a moment when I regretted becoming a policeman and I was sure I could live with the thought of remaining one, instead of going back to Civvy Street to what was far from being a secure future in the aftermath of war. I thought I might find that things in the grocery world, which I had left in 1939, had changed out of all recognition. It was a very important decision that I had to make.

My family had seen very little of me during the past six-and-a-half years and I felt I owed them a debt for the constant worry involved in having a son and brother in the infantry during wartime. The war had lasted nearly seven years and I must have missed a great deal. I knew that I had been a conscientious soldier and had worked hard. I was still only ten-and-a-half stones in weight, but felt very fit.

But the most rewarding thing the war had given me was the great privilege of meeting so many generous, kind-hearted people; soldiers and civilians alike. It had taught me the meaning of comradeship and discipline and had given me priceless memories to think about in my quieter years. The old 6th Green Howards and I had shared, from the very beginning, a new atmosphere among men. I would like to think that, ever so many years later, some of them remember me in their quieter years too, as I most certainly remember them and their ways. They would be the survivors, but the ones who joined their maker will always be as the young men we knew from those days, though I would not like to have kept in touch with any of them. I would rather recall them from 1939 to 1946. For those young men who were never in the forces, I can only say that they do not realise what they have missed.

It came so suddenly – 2 January 1946 – when I was told that I was due for demob on the eighth of the month and was asked if wanted to take advantage of it. Later in the year, the battalion was posted to Palestine to do a tour of duty during the troubles there, so I was pleased I opted for demob, having already had my fill of the sand, flies and food of the Middle East. Nevertheless, the time spent there had been invaluable to me.

The day of 4 January 1946 was when I would pack my kit for the last time. It seemed unbelievable that I would be going home – for good. No more blancoing or polishing of brasses or shining of boots or kit inspection. I had worn nothing but khaki uniform for six-and-a-half years, but I had come through and it was a tremendous feeling.

On the evening of 6 January I did not anticipate what lay ahead of me during the hours to come. All the usual lads – and more – were in the canteen at Wolfsburg and they got me drunk (never before and never since) on rum. We had a rare old singsong of all the old tunes we had all sang, usually on route marches. I will never forget, nor did I ever realise, that the lads held me in such esteem. It was their farewell to me. It was hard to believe that about one hundred young men could pass such an enjoyable evening without the presence of the opposite sex and before the evening had ended they had succeeded in making me drunk. But it was great and I was very touched by such a heartfelt and sincere farewell, and to think that I was going home at last, after all the times I thought the war would never end. They all said what a lucky bugger I was. On 8 January I went to the company office to receive my discharge papers, with a very good commendation, and I left with all kinds of memories of the past going through my head.

We travelled across Germany in army trucks to a transit camp where our papers were checked again – no more bully stew and rice, and the sounds of war had gone for me forever – no longer were we soldiers, just civilians in Khaki.

Travelling across the Channel to Dover, I could not stop thinking about the army and all I had gone through over the years. How many times had I crossed that stretch of water? The most memorable was at the time of Dunkirk. Oh, what memories. From Dover to Catterick Camp in Yorkshire. It was as if I was in a trance. It wouldn't be long now. The routine was simple and we stayed there one night. I was officially discharged and didn't know whether I was sad or glad. Real comradeship was something Civvy Street didn't know about and never would, in the sense that soldiers experienced it in abundance.

At the age of twenty-eight, I handed in my uniform and kit in exchange for a suit and it was all over. My roving had come to an end. What a tremendous impression those six-and-a-half years had made upon my life. It was all a memory. But what a memory; the recollections stored in my head were priceless gems.

I'd like to conclude my recollection by saying that soldiers of the Second World War were a rare breed of men. Boys of nineteen quickly became stout-hearted men of great calibre, who fought without fear for survival against a ruthless enemy – not only the enemy, but the trauma and depravation endured, particularly in the desert, being in action time-after-time, not knowing if they would be blown to pieces. They all came from the upper echelon of mankind. I would always remember them and pray for the souls of the pals we all knew who fell by the wayside, giving their lives.

I must also pay tribute to the nurses and doctors who tended our every care when we were wounded and not to forget the medical teams in the field hospitals. Sailors and RAF boys, Waafs, Wrens and NAAFI girls and Red Cross – all of these people were top drawer. I should also give praise to a group of people who were 'heaven sent' to service people. The ladies of the Salvation Army and the Women's Voluntary Service were the backbone of a group of people who were always there if help or a cup of tea were needed; they were great. Without all these people being mindful of the other's needs, the war would not have reached its successful conclusion. I feel very proud to have served my country and to have lived through this generation of men.

A parting anecdote. In December 1947, I received a Christmas card from Leslie Buckler, the boy who was my orderly in the 22nd Canadian General Hospital. It had been sent to Dundee Royal Infirmary and forwarded to my home address. What a lovely thought from a complete stranger. It was posted in Three Hills, Canada on 10 November and is still amongst my souvenirs.

I often wonder what memories in fifty years' time today's youth will have to look back on. Will they be able to look back with nostalgia to great happenings in their life? The war had taken almost seven years out of my twenties, but had given me experience beyond my wildest dreams and had enabled me to travel to see parts of the world that it would have been highly improbable that I would otherwise have set eyes upon. I thank God I was fortunate enough to endure the war from beginning to end. On so many occasions I could have been killed. I was lucky.

The 'Last Post' still brings a tear to my eye.

The End
Bill Cheall

Epilogue: Back to Normandy, June 1984

IT CAME as an extremely pleasant surprise when, one day as my wife Anne and I were working at my daughter Pauline's house, together with her husband, David, we were having a break and chatting over a cup of coffee and Pauline asked us how we would like a trip to Normandy to join in the 40th D-Day celebrations, and we were to share all expenses.

The visit was constantly in my thoughts until, on 1 June we were off. We had decided to go a week before the celebrations in order to avoid the massive crowds which would be there, and furthermore we wanted to be at home to have a better overall picture of what was taking place by sitting watching television. So 1 June found me once again on a ship going to France across the Channel, but under vastly different conditions to those of forty years ago. I was going to enjoy myself.

Back in 1944, a great multitude of thoughts was going through my mind, so very different. This first day, the beginning of a very sentimental journey, particularly for me, was to be a very special time. It was 1 June 1984, and it was forty long years since the same date in 1944 when I stepped across the threshold of our invasion ship, *Otranto*.

We travelled by hovercraft from Dover to Calais. The last time I had been to Calais was early 1940 when my battalion was part of the British Expeditionary Force.

Our first stop was at Gravelines, a little further up the coast and the scene of our early clashes with the enemy in 1940. Nothing appeared to have changed. The row of small cottages at the roadside was still there. I found the spot where Lieutenant Hewson had been killed and then visited Fort-Mardyck where he is buried. I passed a little time just walking around the place – just thinking.

My next stop was at Bray–Dunes and not a thing had changed here, either. I got out of the car three hundred yards from the edge of the village and walked exactly the same road as I had done all those years ago in 1940 during the retreat. I walked down to the end of the road overlooking the beach, turned left along the road for a hundred yards, then onto the sand dunes and sat down in the same spot where we had dug into the sand into which I ran to escape the Stukas dive-bombing; my thoughts ran riot.

I walked down to the sea and stood looking across the water towards England, visualising everything as it was last time I was there; the ships and the columns of tired and hungry soldiers forming the long queues down to and into the sea, trying to get aboard the small boats which had come fairly close inshore and some of which capsized. All trying to get back to England, only to be killed later in North Africa. All went through my thoughts as I stood there, dreaming of the past. I walked along the beach five miles to the East Mole at Dunkirk, picking up seashells on the way to keep as souvenirs of my visit. I imagined the huge columns of black smoke billowing from the blazing oil tanks.

Retracing my steps, I thought of all the pals I had known at the time, and how many had been killed in various actions after they had got safely back to England, sent to the Middle East and killed.

There was one change to what I remembered, and that was the large gun emplacement which had been erected as part of the Atlantic Wall.

I went in a half-circle from Bray-Dunes by road, covering the same ground over which I had seen the poor refugees being machine gunned by the planes. Then as I headed towards the coast and Bayeux, I could imagine all those thousands of our army vehicles, burnt out or immobilised. I had booked in at the Hotel Lyon D'or at Bayeux where many German officers of senior rank had been in residence during the occupation. Bayeux was decorated, ready for the visits of many dignitaries. British, American and French flags hung from every building and across the streets.

I come upon a plaque on a wall, which declared to all that on 7 June our 50th Division had liberated that city, the first town to be freed. I was so proud that I had been part of it. There was a welcoming sense of friendship and gratitude amongst the French locals.

During my stay, I wandered down to Gold Beach, walked to the sea, turned and walked back up the beach, carried away by the emotion of my racing thoughts about what happened on that very beach, that day, so long ago, when we waded ashore at 0725 hrs.

It was so peaceful, and the amazing thing was that the weather was almost the same – drizzling – but that did not deter me. I was determined not to waste a minute of my time in Normandy. Walking up the beach, there were no mines or booby traps, no shells, machine-gun fire or dead British soldiers. It was tranquil.

We visited the Bayeux war museum and I was enthralled to see such prominent recognition of the fact that our 50th Division had made such an important contribution to the D-Day landings, in liberating the city.

Going across the road to the cemetery which, like all military burial grounds, was magnificently maintained, I wandered along the rows of graves looking for the Green Howard emblem on the headstones. I had brought with me a list of names whose graves I was looking for and one by one I crossed them off the list. I found the last resting-place of our young company commander, Captain Linn, who was killed on the beach within minutes of setting foot on the shore. I found Rufty Hill's grave. You will recall he was killed when the assault craft went over him. He had been such a big strong young man, full of the joy of life. Then I found the grave of our Captain Chambers, who was killed in the cornfield. I found many graves of Green Howards. They had all been good young soldiers and I remembered them as such. I saluted each grave then went and signed the visitor's book, 'Remembered always, a Green Howard.'

All those splendid lives gone. What a great tragedy and waste of human life war is. I know it is said that one cannot live in the past but nor should one forget those young men who paid the supreme sacrifice and it would be hypocritical to forget them. I shall never do that, or how they died. I am not ashamed to look back with sentiment and pride that I served alongside them.

Next stop, Arromanches, also liberated by 50th Division. The museum there, too, had a large display of the Green Howards and 50th Division.

I then stood on the rocks and looked out to sea. Standing like sentinels were the huge blocks of concrete which had once been the Mulberry Harbour, pounded by the sea. When I had last seen the harbour in its entirety, I was on a stretcher being put aboard a hospital ship.

About three-quarters of a mile from there was a spot where our B Company had waded ashore through the surf onto the beach at 0725 hrs on 6 June 1944, and it all came back to me so vividly. D Company on our right, and the spot where Hollis won the only Victoria Cross to be won on D-Day. I saw that knocked-out tank on the beach and all the dead and wounded lads lying around, and the shelling and mortaring. I turned around and could see all those ships at sea. Yes, it was indeed a very traumatic experience to return to France.

Although they do not enter into my story, I also visited all the American beaches and inland, where they had fought – notably, St Mare Eglise and Omaha, which of course was the beach to the right of Gold and where so many brave young Americans met an untimely end. I went to Pont du Hoc and saw the German gun emplacement. Each of the shell holes had been left as they were at the end of D-Day.

While I stood on a rock, looking out to sea, a huge black American came up to me, eyeing me suspiciously. He turned out to be a Secret Service agent and, together with others of his profession, he had been covering the area looking for any characters intent on doing harm to President Reagan who was due for the celebrations. Anyway, after telling him of my visit, he took my hand in a vice-like grip and said he felt privileged to meet an ex-soldier who had taken part in the initial assault on D-Day.

It made my day. It was my last day and I returned home to dream.

I had the opportunity to repeat this memorable visit on the occasion of the 50th D-Day celebrations, when we attended around 6 June 1994, taking part in the official ceremonies and parades in the presence of Her Majesty the Queen. Readers who wish to read my diary for this episode can see it at www.fightingthrough.co.uk.

Names I Will Always Remember

THESE AND other names mentioned in my memoir are shown on a companion web site to this book at www.fightingthrough.co.uk/remembered. Any further information will be gratefully received about all persons mentioned in the book and will be recorded permanently for posterity.

Surname	Rank or First Name	Notes
Beckermeyer	Helmut	German prisoner of war, home town Bremen
Bertram	George	Not known
Betley	Jack	Killed in Sicily
Booth	Ernest	Wounded in Sicily but survived
Bousfield	John	Killed at Wadi Akarit
Bristow	R	Killed in Sicily
Buckler	Leslie	Canadian medical orderly
Burns	Sergeant Frank	Killed on beach, D-Day
Cargill	Jack	Entered the Church, Post-War
Carmichael	Captain	6th batt, M T Officer
Castor	Ivor	Lost an arm at Arnhem. Discharged
Chaffe	Tommy	Not known
Chambers	Captain	Killed in action
Collings	Bill	Killed on HMS *York*
Coughlan	L/Cpl Leslie	Killed Wadi Akarit
Decker	Alfred	German prisoner of war, home town Bremen
Farrand	Lieutenant	Taken prisoner, Gravelines
Foster	Captain	Taken prisoner, Gravelines
Gort	Commander-in-Chief – B.E.F	
Greenwood	Harold	Died 1976
Harrington	Sergeant	Killed in Sicily

Herbert	O.C.	23rd Division – France
Hewson	Lieutenant	Killed at Gravelines
Hill	L/Sergeant Rufty	Drowned, D-Day
Hollis	Sgt Major Stanley	Survived the war. Died 1970
Hughes	Reg Sgt Major	Still living
Hull	Captain	Survived as Major. Died early 80s
Jones	Margaret	Died 1960
Kidd	Captain	Taken prisoner, Gravelines
Lee	Charlie	Killed in Sicily
Linn	Captain	Killed on beach, D-Day
Mill	Alex	Killed in Sicily
Myson	Sergeant	Killed at Wadi Akarit
Owen	Margaret	Died 1958
Oxley	Arthur	Killed at Wadi Akarit
Petch	Major Leslie	Died 1983
Ryan	John	Killed in Sicily
Savage	Donald	Missing RAF
Smith	Corporal	Killed Wadi Akarit
Spooner	Jack	Survived the war
Steel	Lt Col – Battalion Commander	
Wiseman	Mary	From Dufftown, Scotland
Wolf	Dietmar	From Germany

I learned the following from the War Graves Commission:

John Bousfield is buried in Row O, Grave number 11, Beja War Cemetery in Tunisia.

L/Cpl Coughlan's body must have been destroyed after I had left it. His name is on Face 17 Medjez-El-Bab Memorial, Tunisia.

Index